dinnerlamb

THE AUSTRALIAN Women's Weekly

contents

The problem in planning a book like *Dinner Lamb* is not being able to stop coming up with ideas. Tender, tasty and oh-so-tempting, versatile lamb can star as the main ingredient in countless dishes... no wonder we were spoilt for choice when deciding which recipes to include. We hope you agree that our final selection deserves full marks.

Pamela Clark

Food Director

WEEKNIGHTS

When you're pushed for time, quick-cooking lamb cuts are the answer. From start to finish, all of these dishes can be on the table in less than an hour.

spicy sausage pasta bake

PREPARATION TIME 15 MINUTES **COOKING TIME** 35 MINUTES

Tortiglioni, a straight tubular pasta with grooves on the exterior, works well when baked with a chunky sauce, such as this one. You can substitute it with rigatoni or ziti, if you like, but anything less substantial will get lost amid the hearty sausage and vegetable melange.

375g tortiglioni
6 spicy lamb sausages (900g)
1 medium brown onion (150g), chopped coarsely
1 small eggplant (230g), chopped coarsely
2 medium red capsicums (400g), chopped coarsely
3 small green zucchini (270g), chopped coarsely
700g bottled tomato pasta sauce
½ cup coarsely chopped fresh basil
2 cups (200g) grated pizza cheese

1. Preheat oven to moderate (180°C/160°C fan-forced).
2. Cook pasta in large saucepan of boiling water, uncovered, until just tender; drain.
3. Meanwhile, cook sausages in large non-stick frying pan until just cooked through. Drain on absorbent paper.
4. Cook onion, eggplant, capsicum and zucchini, stirring, in same pan until just tender.
5. Cut sausages into 2cm slices; add to vegetables in pan with sauce and basil, stir to combine.
6. Combine pasta and sausage mixture in deep 3-litre (12-cup) casserole dish; sprinkle with cheese. Bake, uncovered, in moderate oven about 20 minutes or until browned lightly.

serves 6
per serving 36.3g total fat (16.5g saturated fat); 3453kJ (826 cal); 67.7g carbohydrate; 57.6g protein; 7.5g fibre

lamb and rosemary pies with peas

PREPARATION TIME 20 MINUTES **COOKING TIME** 25 MINUTES

1 Heat half of the oil in large saucepan; cook lamb, in batches, uncovered, until browned all over. Heat remaining oil in same pan; cook onion, stirring, until soft. Add flour; cook, stirring, until mixture bubbles and thickens. Gradually add wine, stock, paste and rosemary leaves; stir until mixture boils and thickens. Stir in lamb; cool 10 minutes.

2 Preheat oven to moderately hot (200°C/180°C fan-forced). Oil four holes of 6-hole (¾-cup/180ml) texas muffin pan.

3 Cut two 13cm rounds from opposite corners of each pastry sheet; cut two 9cm rounds from remaining corners of each sheet. Place larger rounds in prepared holes to cover bases and sides; trim any excess pastry, prick bases with fork.

4 Spoon lamb mixture into pastry cases; brush around edges with a little egg. Top pies with smaller rounds; gently press around edges to seal. Brush pies with remaining egg; press one rosemary sprig into top of each pie.

5 Bake pies, uncovered, in moderately hot oven about 15 minutes or until browned lightly. Stand 5 minutes in pan before serving.

6 Meanwhile, heat butter in medium saucepan; add peas, juice and the water, cook, uncovered, stirring occasionally, about 5 minutes or until peas are just tender.

2 tablespoons olive oil
400g diced lamb
4 baby onions (100g), quartered
1 tablespoon plain flour
¼ cup (60ml) dry red wine
¾ cup (180ml) beef stock
1 tablespoon tomato paste
1 tablespoon fresh rosemary leaves
2 sheets ready-rolled puff pastry
1 egg, beaten lightly
4 fresh rosemary sprigs
20g butter
2½ cups (300g) frozen peas
1 tablespoon lemon juice
½ cup (125ml) water

serves 4
per serving 42.7g total fat (18.6g saturated fat); 2868kJ (686 cal); 40.4g carbohydrate; 33.1g protein; 6.1g fibre

lemon and garlic cutlets with broad bean, mixed pea and fetta salad

PREPARATION TIME 30 MINUTES **COOKING TIME** 15 MINUTES

If you can find fresh broad beans, buy about 500g in their pods for this recipe. First, peel them then slit along the rounded back of each bean to remove the hard, grey outer shell. Blanch or microwave the remaining tiny green beans until just tender.

2 tablespoons olive oil
1 tablespoon finely grated lemon rind
2 tablespoons lemon juice
2 cloves garlic, crushed
12 french-trimmed cutlets (600g)
1⅓ cups (225g) frozen broad beans
⅔ cup (80g) frozen baby peas
200g snow peas, trimmed, sliced thinly
1 cup coarsely chopped fresh basil
150g fetta cheese, crumbled
1 cup (150g) seeded kalamata olives

LEMON DRESSING

2 tablespoons lemon juice
¼ cup (60ml) olive oil
1 teaspoon dijon mustard

1. Combine oil, rind, juice and garlic in large bowl; add cutlets, turn to coat in mixture.
2. Boil, steam or microwave beans and peas, separately, until just tender; drain. Rinse under cold water; drain. Peel away grey-coloured outer shells from broad beans; combine beans and peas in large bowl.
3. Meanwhile, place ingredients for lemon dressing in screw-top jar; shake well.
4. Cook cutlets, in batches, on heated oiled grill plate (or grill or barbecue) until browned both sides and cooked as desired.
5. Place snow peas, basil, cheese, olives and half of the dressing in bowl with beans and peas; toss gently. Serve salad topped with cutlets; drizzle with remaining dressing. Sprinkle with a little finely grated lemon rind, if desired.

serves 4
per serving 45.2g total fat (14.9g saturated fat); 2424kJ (580 cal); 17.1g carbohydrate; 27.1g protein; 6.7g fibre

bacon-wrapped chops with baby potatoes in olive pesto

PREPARATION TIME 20 MINUTES **COOKING TIME** 20 MINUTES

8 loin chops (800g)
4 bacon rashers (280g), rind removed, halved lengthways
⅓ cup (80ml) olive oil
4 medium egg tomatoes (300g), halved
800g baby new potatoes, halved
1 cup firmly packed fresh basil leaves
1 tablespoon lemon juice
¼ cup (60ml) buttermilk
½ cup (60g) seeded green olives
¼ cup (40g) toasted pine nuts

1. Wrap each chop around the outside with one strip of the bacon; securing each with a toothpick.
2. Heat 1 tablespoon of the oil in large frying pan; cook chops, in batches, until browned both sides and cooked as desired. Remove toothpicks, cover chops; stand 5 minutes.
3. Meanwhile, cook tomato in same pan, cut-side down, until soft. Boil, steam or microwave potato until tender; drain.
4. Blend or process remaining oil with basil, juice and buttermilk until mixture forms a smooth paste. Add olives and pine nuts; process pesto until just combined.
5. Place potato and pesto in large bowl; toss gently to combine. Divide potato, chops and tomato among serving plates. Serve with tomato chutney, if desired.

serves 4
per serving 44g total fat (11.3g saturated fat); 3001kJ (718 cal); 33.4g carbohydrate; 46.8g protein; 6.3g fibre

Always press the trimmed basil leaves firmly into a measuring cup so that the proportion of the herb to the other pesto ingredients is correct: too little basil will give the paste a watery texture and a taste that's more of olive than herb.

SKEWERS

Each of these recipes makes eight kebabs; serve with steamed rice or warmed pitta bread, if desired. Soak bamboo skewers in cold water for at least 1 hour before using to prevent them scorching and splintering.

rosemary and garlic kebabs

PREPARATION TIME 20 MINUTES
COOKING TIME 20 MINUTES

8 x 15cm stalks fresh rosemary
1 clove garlic, crushed
1 tablespoon lemon juice
1 tablespoon olive oil
500g diced lamb

1 Pull enough leaves from bottom of rosemary stalks to make 2 tablespoons of finely chopped leaves; toss in small bowl with garlic, juice and oil.
2 Thread lamb onto rosemary stalk skewers; brush with rosemary oil mixture.
3 Cook kebabs on heated oiled grill plate (or grill or barbecue) until browned all over and cooked as desired.

per serving 15.6g total fat (5.7g saturated fat); 1024kJ (245 cal); 0.3g carbohydrate; 26.2g protein; 0.1g fibre

yakitori

PREPARATION TIME 20 MINUTES
COOKING TIME 20 MINUTES

½ cup (125ml) japanese soy sauce
½ cup (125ml) sake
¼ cup (60ml) mirin
2 tablespoons white sugar
500g diced lamb
1 medium carrot (120g), sliced thinly
6 green onions, cut into 3cm lengths

1 Combine sauce, sake, mirin and sugar in small saucepan; bring to a boil. Reduce heat; simmer, uncovered, until sauce reduces by a third. Cool 10 minutes.
2 Meanwhile, thread lamb, carrot and onion, alternately, onto skewers.
3 Cook kebabs on heated oiled grill plate (or grill or barbecue), brushing with half of the sauce occasionally, until browned all over and cooked as desired. Serve yakitori with remaining sauce.

per serving 11.1g total fat (5g saturated fat); 1229kJ (294 cal); 12.1g carbohydrate; 28.4g protein; 1.1g fibre

thai red curry skewers

PREPARATION TIME 20 MINUTES
COOKING TIME 20 MINUTES

2 tablespoons thai red curry paste

1 tablespoon fish sauce

1 tablespoon brown sugar

1 tablespoon lime juice

500g diced lamb

1 medium red capsicum (200g), diced into 2cm pieces

1 lime, cut into 8 wedges

1 Combine paste, sauce, sugar and juice in small bowl.
2 Thread lamb and capsicum, alternately, onto skewers; thread one lime wedge on each skewer. Brush skewers with half of the curry paste mixture.
3 Cook kebabs on heated oiled grill plate (or grill or barbecue), brushing with remaining curry paste mixture occasionally, until browned all over and cooked as desired.

per serving 14.7g total fat (5.4g saturated fat); 1124kJ (269 cal); 6.1g carbohydrate; 27.9g protein; 2g fibre

haloumi and allspice kebabs

PREPARATION TIME 20 MINUTES
COOKING TIME 20 MINUTES

½ teaspoon ground allspice

1 teaspoon cracked black pepper

1 clove garlic, crushed

2 tablespoons lemon juice

2 tablespoons olive oil

500g diced lamb

200g haloumi cheese, diced into 2cm pieces

1 Place allspice, pepper, garlic, juice and oil in medium bowl; add lamb, turn to coat in mixture. Thread lamb and cheese, alternately, onto skewers.
2 Cook kebabs on heated oiled grill plate (or grill or barbecue) until browned all over and cooked as desired.

per serving 28.7g total fat (11.8g saturated fat); 1710kJ (409 cal); 1.5g carbohydrate; 36.9g protein; 0.1g fibre

chilli rice noodles with bok choy

PREPARATION TIME 20 MINUTES **COOKING TIME** 15 MINUTES

Fresh rice noodles are found in the refrigerated sections of supermarkets as well as in Asian grocery stores. Because they're fresh and not dried, they do not need to be reconstituted by cooking, nor do they require a lengthy soaking time.

400g fresh thin rice noodles
1 tablespoon peanut oil
500g lamb mince
3 cloves garlic, crushed
2 fresh small red thai chillies, chopped finely
400g bok choy, sliced thinly
2 tablespoons tamari
1 tablespoon fish sauce
2 tablespoons kecap manis
4 green onions, sliced thinly
1 cup firmly packed fresh thai basil leaves
3 cups (240g) bean sprouts

1. Place noodles in medium heatproof bowl; cover with boiling water, separate with fork, drain.
2. Heat oil in wok; stir-fry mince until browned. Add garlic and chilli; stir-fry until fragrant. Add noodles, bok choy, tamari, sauce and kecap manis; stir-fry until bok choy just wilts.
3. Remove from heat; stir in onion, basil and sprouts. Serve topped with sliced chilli, if desired.

serves 4
per serving 14.4g total fat (4.7g saturated fat); 1877kJ (449 cal); 44.5g carbohydrate; 34.3g protein; 5.3g fibre

char-grilled cutlets with white bean puree and tapenade

PREPARATION TIME 20 MINUTES **COOKING TIME** 25 MINUTES

2 x 400g cans white beans, rinsed, drained
1 cup (250ml) chicken stock
1 clove garlic, crushed
1 tablespoon cream
2 tablespoons lemon juice
2 tablespoons olive oil
¼ cup (60g) black olive tapenade
12 french-trimmed cutlets (600g)
300g baby spinach leaves

1 Combine beans and stock in medium saucepan; bring to a boil. Reduce heat; simmer, uncovered, about 15 minutes or until liquid is absorbed. Transfer to medium bowl; mash beans with garlic, cream, juice and one tablespoon of the oil until smooth. Cover to keep warm.
2 Meanwhile, combine tapenade with remaining oil in small bowl.
3 Cook cutlets, in batches, on heated oiled grill plate (or grill or barbecue) until browned both sides and cooked as desired; cover to keep warm.
4 Boil, steam or microwave spinach until just wilted; drain.
5 Divide bean puree, spinach and cutlets among serving plates; drizzle with tapenade mixture.

Many varieties of white beans are available canned, among them cannellini, butter and haricot beans: any of these is suitable for this puree. Drain beans then rinse well under cold water before using them. We find that cooking them briefly with a little liquid results in a more luscious, creamier puree.

serves 4
per serving 25.6g total fat (9g saturated fat); 1438kJ (344 cal); 8g carbohydrate; 21.1g protein; 5g fibre

mediterranean vegetable-filled steaks

PREPARATION TIME 25 MINUTES **COOKING TIME** 15 MINUTES

Kitchen string can be put to a-hundred-and-one uses when you're cooking, but be certain to use an all-cotton string and not one made from synthetic material: your food will not be improved by the taste of molten plastic.

4 butterfly lamb steaks (360g)
8 fresh basil leaves
8 (100g) marinated quartered artichoke hearts, drained
⅔ cup (100g) drained semi-dried tomatoes
150g bocconcini, sliced thinly

ROCKET AND RED ONION SALAD
2 tablespoons olive oil
1 tablespoon lemon juice
1 teaspoon dijon mustard
100g rocket leaves
½ cup loosely packed fresh basil leaves
1 medium red onion (170g), sliced thinly
1 tablespoon baby capers, rinsed, drained

1 Using meat mallet, gently pound steaks between sheets of plastic wrap until 1cm thick. Place two basil leaves on one half of each steak; top each with two artichoke quarters, a quarter of the tomato and a quarter of the cheese. Fold each steak over filling; tie with kitchen string.
2 Cook steaks on heated oiled grill plate (or grill or barbecue) until browned both sides and cooked as desired.
3 Meanwhile, make rocket and red onion salad.
4 Serve steaks with salad.

ROCKET AND RED ONION SALAD Place oil, juice and mustard in screw-top jar; shake well. Place remaining ingredients in large bowl with dressing; toss gently.

serves 4
per serving 25.4g total fat (9.2g saturated fat); 1672kJ (400 cal); 12g carbohydrate; 30.2g protein; 4.9g fibre

butterflied steaks with nam jim and cucumber and asparagus salad

PREPARATION TIME 25 MINUTES **COOKING TIME** 15 MINUTES

Shallots, also called french shallots, golden shallots or eschalots, are small, elongated members of the onion family that grow in tight clusters, similarly to garlic. Singapore noodles are cryovac-packed, pre-cooked wheat noodles that are best described as a thinner version of hokkien noodles, with which they can be substituted.

400g singapore noodles

6 butterflied lamb steaks (540g)

NAM JIM

3 fresh long red chillies

3 fresh small red thai chillies

2cm piece fresh ginger (10g), grated

1 shallot (25g), quartered

2 cloves garlic, quartered

⅓ cup (80ml) lime juice

2 tablespoons fish sauce

¼ cup (35g) finely chopped roasted unsalted peanuts

1 tablespoon finely chopped fresh coriander

CUCUMBER AND ASPARAGUS SALAD

500g asparagus, trimmed, cut into 2cm lengths

1 telegraph cucumber (400g), seeded, sliced thickly

½ cup firmly packed fresh coriander leaves

1 cup (50g) toasted flaked coconut

1 tablespoon peanut oil

1. Make nam jim. Make cucumber and asparagus salad.
2. Place noodles in large heatproof bowl, cover with boiling water; stand until just tender, drain. Stir in 2 tablespoons of the nam jim.
3. Meanwhile, cook steaks on heated oiled grill plate (or grill or barbecue), in batches, until browned both sides and cooked as desired. Slice lamb thickly.
4. Divide noodles among serving dishes; serve with lamb, salad and individual bowls of nam jim.

NAM JIM Blend or process chillies, ginger, shallot, garlic, juice and sauce, pulsing, until mixture is chopped finely. Stir in nuts and coriander.

CUCUMBER AND ASPARAGUS SALAD Boil, steam or microwave asparagus until just tender; drain. Rinse under cold water; drain. Combine asparagus in medium bowl with remaining ingredients; toss gently.

serves 4
per serving 30g total fat (14.4g saturated fat); 2851kJ (682 cal); 56.7g carbohydrate; 45.1g protein; 7.3g fibre

tamarind-glazed rack with tat soi and orange salad

PREPARATION TIME 10 MINUTES **COOKING TIME** 25 MINUTES

Tat soi's dark-green, spoon-shaped leaves are usually eaten raw in salads, but can also be combined with other Asian greens in soups, curries and stir-fries. Also known as rosette, pak choy and chinese flat cabbage, it is a member of the same family as bok choy, and has the same mild flavour.

You need to buy a small head of tat soi for this recipe.

¼ cup (60ml) tamarind concentrate
¼ cup (60ml) orange juice
2 teaspoons sesame oil
1 tablespoon brown sugar
4 x 4 french-trimmed cutlet racks (600g)
2 large oranges (600g)
100g tat soi leaves
100g shiitake mushrooms, sliced thickly

1 Preheat oven to moderately hot (200°C/180°C fan-forced).
2 Combine tamarind, juice, oil and sugar in small saucepan; reserve 2 tablespoons of the mixture in large bowl. Bring remaining mixture in pan to a boil. Reduce heat; simmer, uncovered, about 2 minutes or until mixture thickens slightly.
3 Place lamb on metal rack inside large shallow baking dish; brush hot tamarind glaze over racks. Cook, uncovered, in moderately hot oven about 20 minutes or until racks are cooked as desired. Cover racks; stand 10 minutes.
4 Meanwhile, segment oranges over reserved tamarind mixture in bowl. Add tat soi and mushrooms; toss gently.
5 Cut each lamb rack in half; place two halves on each serving plate, serve with salad.

serves 4
per serving 15.4g total fat (6.2g saturated fat); 1132kJ (271 cal); 15.7g carbohydrate; 17.7g protein; 3.4g fibre

paprika-dusted loin chops served with greek salad

PREPARATION TIME 15 MINUTES **COOKING TIME** 10 MINUTES

8 loin chops (800g)
2 teaspoons sweet paprika
¼ cup (60ml) olive oil
1 medium red capsicum (200g), chopped coarsely
1 medium green capsicum (200g), chopped coarsely
2 medium tomatoes (300g), chopped coarsely
200g fetta cheese, diced into 2cm pieces
1 tablespoon lemon juice
¼ cup firmly packed fresh flat-leaf parsley leaves

1 Sprinkle chops with paprika. Heat 1 tablespoon of the oil in large frying pan; cook chops until browned both sides and cooked as desired. Cover chops; stand 5 minutes.
2 Meanwhile, combine capsicums, tomato, cheese, juice, parsley and remaining oil in large bowl; toss gently.
3 Divide salad and chops among serving plates; serve with lemon wedges, if desired.

serves 4
per serving 38.6g total fat (15.9g saturated fat); 2236kJ (535 cal); 4.4g carbohydrate; 42.8g protein; 1.9g fibre

There are more than 40 varieties of the paprika pepper grown in Turkey, Hungary, Iran and Spain, but the differences among them are very subtle. We generally have four types of paprika at most in our cupboards – smoked, fiery hot, sweet and bittersweet.

madras curry

PREPARATION TIME 10 MINUTES **COOKING TIME** 30 MINUTES

Butternut pumpkin contains no fat, is low in kilojoules and rich in beta-carotene and vitamin C. A variety of the gramma family, the butternut has an elongated bell shape, a sweet, nutty flavour and a fairly dry texture. It is very popular and versatile. It can star as an ingredient in a soup, risotto or warm salad, and it's fab mashed then eaten on its own or made into gnocchi, a sweet pie, scones or bread.

Backstrap is sold as eye of loin by some butchers.

500g butternut pumpkin, diced into 2cm pieces
200g green beans, chopped coarsely
2 tablespoons vegetable oil
600g backstrap, diced into 2cm pieces
1 medium brown onion (150g), chopped finely
2 cloves garlic, crushed
½ cup (150g) madras curry paste
1 cup (250ml) beef stock
425g can crushed tomatoes
2 cups (400g) basmati rice
1 cup (250ml) buttermilk
½ cup coarsely chopped fresh coriander

1. Boil, steam or microwave pumpkin and beans, separately, until just tender; drain. Rinse beans under cold water; drain.
2. Meanwhile, heat half of the oil in wok; stir-fry lamb, in batches, until just browned.
3. Heat remaining oil in same wok; stir-fry onion and garlic until onion softens. Add paste; stir-fry until fragrant. Return lamb to wok with stock and undrained tomatoes; bring to a boil. Add pumpkin, reduce heat; simmer curry, covered, stirring occasionally, 10 minutes.
4. Meanwhile, cook rice in large saucepan of boiling water, uncovered, until just tender; drain.
5. Add beans and buttermilk to curry; stir over low heat until heated through. Remove from heat; stir in coriander. Serve curry with rice, sprinkle with extra chopped fresh corriander, if desired.

serves 4
per serving 36.9g total fat (9.7g saturated fat); 3829kJ (916 cal); 97.4g carbohydrate; 47.9g protein; 9.1g fibre

schnitzel with caper herb mash and anchovy mayonnaise

PREPARATION TIME 15 MINUTES **COOKING TIME** 20 MINUTES

4 x 150g lamb steaks

¼ cup (35g) plain flour

2 eggs, beaten lightly

1 tablespoon milk

2 cups (140g) stale breadcrumbs

½ cup (40g) finely grated parmesan cheese

vegetable oil, for shallow-frying

CAPER HERB MASH

1kg large potatoes, chopped coarsely

½ cup (125ml) cream, warmed

50g butter, melted

2 tablespoons baby capers, rinsed, drained

2 tablespoons finely chopped fresh chives

¼ cup coarsely chopped fresh flat-leaf parsley

ANCHOVY MAYONNAISE

½ cup (150g) whole-egg mayonnaise

4 anchovy fillets, drained, chopped finely

1 tablespoon lemon juice

1 tablespoon warm water

1 Using meat mallet, pound each steak between sheets of plastic wrap until 5mm thick. Place flour in medium shallow bowl; whisk egg and milk in separate medium shallow bowl. Combine breadcrumbs and cheese in a third medium shallow bowl. Coat schnitzels, one at a time, in flour, then egg mixture, and finally breadcrumb mixture. Place schnitzels, in single layer, on tray. Cover; refrigerate.
2 Make caper herb mash.
3 Meanwhile, whisk ingredients for anchovy mayonnaise in small bowl until combined.
4 Heat oil in large frying pan; shallow-fry schnitzels, in batches, until browned both sides and cooked as desired. Drain on absorbent paper; cover to keep warm.
5 Divide caper herb mash and schnitzels among serving plates; drizzle with anchovy mayonnaise.

CAPER HERB MASH Boil, steam or microwave potato until tender; drain. Mash potato in large bowl with cream and butter; cover to keep warm. Stir in capers and herbs just before serving.

serves 4
per serving 70.4g total fat (28.2g saturated fat); 4615kJ (1104 cal); 66.7g carbohydrate; 51.6g protein; 5.7g fibre

backstrap with celeriac mash and watercress

PREPARATION TIME 25 MINUTES **COOKING TIME** 20 MINUTES

Celeriac may not be the prettiest of vegies, but this knobbly brown tuber is quite delicious. It has a white flesh with a subtle celery flavour and, when mashed, has the creaminess of potato. Keep peeled celeriac in acidulated water before deep-frying, boiling or eating it raw.

1.5kg celeriac, trimmed, chopped coarsely
500g potatoes, chopped coarsely
40g butter, softened
½ cup (125ml) cream
1 clove garlic, crushed
2 teaspoons coarsely chopped fresh rosemary
¼ cup (60ml) olive oil
800g backstrap
2 tablespoons balsamic vinegar
300g watercress, trimmed

1. Boil, steam or microwave celeriac and potato until tender; drain. Mash celeriac and potato in large bowl with butter and cream; cover to keep warm.
2. Meanwhile, combine garlic, rosemary and 1 tablespoon of the oil in large bowl; add lamb, turn to coat in mixture. Heat large non-stick frying pan; cook lamb, uncovered, until browned both sides and cooked as desired. Cover lamb; stand 10 minutes then slice thickly.
3. Combine remaining oil and vinegar in small jug. Place watercress with half of the dressing in medium bowl; toss gently.
4. Serve lamb with celeriac mash and watercress; drizzle with remaining dressing.

serves 4
per serving 51.6g total fat (22.9g saturated fat); 3198kJ (765 cal); 26.4g carbohydrate; 49.2g protein; 12.7g fibre

fetta, spinach and prosciutto lamb rolls with herbed kipflers

PREPARATION TIME 20 MINUTES **COOKING TIME** 20 MINUTES

500g kipfler potatoes, halved lengthways
20g butter
1 tablespoon finely chopped fresh flat-leaf parsley
12 slices prosciutto (180g)
20g baby spinach leaves
160g fetta cheese, sliced thinly
4 x 200g pieces backstrap
1 tablespoon olive oil

1 Boil, steam or microwave potato until tender; drain. Toss in large bowl with butter and parsley; cover to keep warm.
2 Meanwhile, slightly overlap three slices of the prosciutto, side by side, on board; layer with a quarter of the spinach, a quarter of the cheese and one piece of the lamb. Starting from narrow end of prosciutto slices, roll carefully to completely enclose lamb. Repeat with remaining prosciutto, spinach, cheese and lamb.
3 Heat oil in large frying pan; cook lamb rolls about 15 minutes or until browned all over and cooked as desired. Cover lamb; stand 10 minutes. Serve lamb sliced thickly with herbed potato and, if desired, a salad of mixed baby leaves.

serves 4
per serving 38.3g total fat (18.4g saturated fat); 2725kJ (652 cal); 16.9g carbohydrate; 60.3g protein; 2.7g fibre

Prosciutto is a kind of Italian ham: salted, air-cured and aged, it is usually eaten uncooked. There are many styles of prosciutto, one of the best being Parma ham, and it's worth it to spend a little more and buy the best quality you can afford.

caramelised onion, pumpkin and lamb pizza

PREPARATION TIME 10 MINUTES **COOKING TIME** 45 MINUTES

Invented in the 1980s by an Italian-American who based his product on a traditional Italian feast-day bread, pre-baked pizza bases are a boon to the weeknight cook. Pitta bread can also be used, and who among us has not made individual pizzas from split English muffins?

1 tablespoon olive oil
2 large brown onions (400g), sliced thinly
600g piece pumpkin, sliced thinly
2 x 335g pizza bases
½ cup (130g) bottled tomato pasta sauce
250g bocconcini, sliced thinly
400g lamb fillets
50g baby rocket leaves

1. Preheat oven to very hot (240°C/220°C fan-forced).
2. Heat oil in medium non-stick saucepan; cook onion, covered, over low heat, stirring occasionally, about 20 minutes or until caramelised.
3. Meanwhile, place pumpkin, in single layer, on lightly oiled oven tray; roast, uncovered, in very hot oven, until just tender.
4. Place pizza bases on oven trays; spread with sauce. Divide cheese and pumpkin between pizzas. Cook, uncovered, in very hot oven about 15 minutes or until pumpkin is browned lightly.
5. Meanwhile, cook lamb, uncovered, in large lightly oiled frying pan over very high heat until cooked as desired. Cover lamb; stand 5 minutes then slice thinly.
6. Serve pizzas topped with caramelised onion, lamb and rocket.

serves 4
per serving 30.1g total fat (12.1g saturated fat); 3733kJ (893 cal); 103.7g carbohydrate; 51.5g protein; 9.8g fibre

fajitas with guacamole and salsa cruda

PREPARATION TIME 30 MINUTES **COOKING TIME** 15 MINUTES

1 Combine garlic, juice, cumin and oil in large bowl; add lamb, stir to coat in mixture. Cover; refrigerate.
2 Make guacamole.
3 Combine ingredients for salsa cruda in small bowl.
4 Cook lamb, in batches, in heated oiled frying pan, stirring, until browned all over and cooked as desired. Cover to keep warm. Cook capsicums and onion, in batches, in same pan, stirring, until just softened.
5 Meanwhile, heat tortillas according to instructions on packet.
6 Return lamb and capsicum mixture to pan; stir gently over medium heat until hot. Divide fajita mixture among serving plates; serve with tortillas, guacamole and salsa cruda.

GUACAMOLE Coarsely chop avocado over small bowl; add remaining ingredients, stir gently to combine.

serves 4
per serving 37.5g total fat (10.4g saturated fat); 3227kJ (772 cal); 62.3g carbohydrate; 45.8g protein; 8.4g fibre

3 cloves garlic, crushed

¼ cup (60ml) lemon juice

2 teaspoons ground cumin

1 tablespoon olive oil

600g lamb strips

1 large red capsicum (350g), sliced thickly

1 large green capsicum (350g), sliced thickly

1 medium yellow capsicum (200g), sliced thickly

1 large red onion (300g), sliced thickly

8 large flour tortillas

GUACAMOLE

1 large avocado (320g)

¼ cup finely chopped fresh coriander

1 tablespoon lime juice

1 small white onion (80g), chopped finely

SALSA CRUDA

2 medium tomatoes (300g), seeded, chopped finely

1 fresh long red chilli, chopped finely

½ cup coarsely chopped fresh coriander

1 clove garlic, crushed

1 small white onion (80g), chopped finely

2 tablespoons lime juice

liver, mushroom and bacon pies with shoestring chips

PREPARATION TIME 15 MINUTES **COOKING TIME** 30 MINUTES

Turn a ramekin upside down on one corner of the pastry sheet and cut around it to make each pie "cap". You'll easily get four from the one sheet, with enough left over to make tiny leaves or stars to decorate each pie's cover, if you desire.

500g lamb liver
2 tablespoons olive oil
1 clove garlic, crushed
1 medium brown onion (150g), chopped finely
4 bacon rashers (280g), rind removed, chopped coarsely
200g button mushrooms, quartered
2 tablespoons plain flour
½ cup (125ml) dry red wine
1½ cups (375ml) beef stock
1kg packet frozen shoestring chips
1 sheet ready-rolled butter puff pastry
1 egg yolk
1 tablespoon milk

1. Preheat oven to hot (220°C/200°C fan-forced). Line oven tray with baking paper.
2. Discard membrane and any fat from liver; chop coarsely. Heat half of the oil in large non-stick frying pan; cook liver, in batches, over high heat until browned and cooked as desired.
3. Heat remaining oil in same pan; cook garlic, onion, bacon and mushrooms, stirring, until onion softens. Add flour; cook, stirring, until mixture thickens and bubbles. Gradually add wine and stock; stir until mixture boils and thickens. Return liver to pan.
4. Meanwhile, cook chips, in hot oven, according to packet instructions.
5. Cut four 9.5cm rounds from pastry sheet; place on prepared tray, brush with combined egg and milk. Bake, uncovered, in hot oven with chips for about 5 minutes or until rounds are browned lightly.
6. Divide liver mixture among four 1¼-cup (310ml) ramekins; top with rounds, serve with chips.

serves 4
per serving 60.2g total fat (13.4g saturated fat); 5543kJ (1326 cal); 136.9g carbohydrate; 53.3g protein; 14.1g fibre

chilli and paprika seared steak with tabbouleh

PREPARATION TIME 30 MINUTES (PLUS STANDING TIME) **COOKING TIME** 10 MINUTES

1 clove garlic, crushed
1 teaspoon dried chilli flakes
1 tablespoon sweet paprika
2 teaspoons ground coriander
1 teaspoon ground cumin
1 tablespoon finely chopped fresh mint
2 tablespoons hot water
4 x 150g lamb steaks

TABBOULEH
¼ cup (40g) burghul
2½ cups coarsely chopped fresh flat-leaf parsley
½ cup coarsely chopped fresh mint
½ cup coarsely chopped fresh coriander
3 medium tomatoes (450g), seeded, chopped coarsely
1 medium red onion (170g), chopped finely
⅔ cup (160ml) lemon juice
⅔ cup (160ml) olive oil

1 Make tabbouleh.
2 Combine garlic, spices, mint and the water in medium bowl; add steaks, turn to coat in mixture. Cook steaks on heated oiled grill plate (or grill or barbecue) until browned both sides and cooked as desired. Cover steaks; stand 5 minutes.
3 Serve steaks with tabbouleh.

TABBOULEH Cover burghul with cold water in small bowl; stand about 10 minutes or until burghul softens, drain. Using hands, squeeze out excess water then combine burghul in medium bowl with herbs, tomato and onion. Combine juice and oil in screw-top jar, shake well; drizzle over tabbouleh, toss gently.

serves 4
per serving 44g total fat (8.4g saturated fat); 2195kJ (525 cal); 11.5g carbohydrate; 20.8g protein; 6.4g fibre

Fleshy, tender leaves like mint (and basil and sage) darken and become limp quickly once they've been chopped so it's a good idea not to handle them until the last possible minute, particularly if they're being used raw. Above, you can see the difference in whole leaves, coarsely chopped then finely chopped mint. In a salad like tabbouleh, it's best to leave the leaves somewhat large so that they maintain their textural crispness and aren't lost amid the other herbs.

lamb, spinach and spiced peach salad

PREPARATION TIME 20 MINUTES **COOKING TIME** 15 MINUTES

There are many white wine vinegars available that have had fruit or herbs macerated in them. Raspberry is one of the most common varieties, and it can be used in a great many ways other than as part of a vinaigrette. Sprinkle it over a bowl of cooked vegetables or a fresh fruit salad to bring up the flavours and add a note of piquancy, or use it in a marinade or sauce for meat, poultry or game – it's particularly suited to duck.

20g butter
1 teaspoon ground coriander
½ teaspoon ground cardamom
¼ teaspoon ground cinnamon
3 medium peaches (450g), peeled, sliced thickly
2 tablespoons brown sugar
1 tablespoon raspberry vinegar
800g backstrap
1 large red onion (300g), sliced thinly
150g snow peas, trimmed, sliced thinly
150g baby spinach leaves
2 fresh long red chillies, sliced thinly

RASPBERRY DRESSING
120g raspberries
2 tablespoons raspberry vinegar
2 tablespoons olive oil
1 teaspoon sugar
1 teaspoon dijon mustard

1. Melt butter in large frying pan; cook spices, stirring, until fragrant. Add peach; cook, stirring, about 2 minutes or until just tender. Add sugar and vinegar; cook, stirring, until sugar dissolves. Remove peach from pan with slotted spoon; place in large bowl.
2. Add lamb to sugar mixture in pan; cook, uncovered, over low heat until browned both sides and cooked as desired. Cover lamb; stand 10 minutes then slice thickly.
3. Meanwhile, blend or process ingredients for raspberry dressing until smooth.
4. Combine lamb and remaining ingredients in bowl with peach; toss gently. Serve salad drizzled with dressing.

serves 4
per serving 31.3g total fat (12g saturated fat); 2303kJ (551 cal); 21.3g carbohydrate; 46g protein; 5.6g fibre

za'atar-grilled lamb with fattoush

PREPARATION TIME 25 MINUTES **COOKING TIME** 10 MINUTES

1 clove garlic, crushed

1 teaspoon sweet paprika

1 tablespoon sumac

1 teaspoon finely chopped fresh oregano

1 tablespoon water

1 tablespoon olive oil

800g backstrap

FATTOUSH

1 large pitta

3 lebanese cucumbers (390g), seeded, chopped coarsely

3 medium tomatoes (450g), seeded, chopped coarsely

5 trimmed red radishes (75g), sliced thinly

3 green onions, sliced thickly

1 cup coarsely chopped fresh flat-leaf parsley

1 cup coarsely chopped fresh mint

1 baby cos lettuce, torn

2 tablespoons sumac

⅓ cup (80ml) lemon juice

¼ cup (60ml) olive oil

1. Combine garlic, paprika, sumac, oregano, the water and oil in medium bowl; add lamb, turn to coat in mixture.
2. Cook lamb on heated oiled grill plate (or grill or barbecue) until browned both sides and cooked as desired. Cover lamb; stand 10 minutes then slice thickly.
3. Meanwhile, make fattoush.
4. Serve lamb with fattoush.

FATTOUSH Split pitta in half; toast pitta under preheated grill. Combine cucumber, tomato, radish, onion, herbs and lettuce in large bowl. Place sumac, juice and oil in screw-top jar; shake well. Pour dressing over salad; toss gently. Break pitta into small pieces over salad just before serving.

serves 4

per serving 36.8g total fat (10.7g saturated fat); 2437kJ (583 cal); 16.4g carbohydrate; 46.7g protein; 5.5g fibre

hokkien noodle stir-fry

PREPARATION TIME 15 MINUTES **COOKING TIME** 15 MINUTES

Hokkien noodles are fresh wheat noodles, also called shanghai or stir-fry. They don't need to be rehydrated in boiling water before use – give them a quick douse in hot water to rinse away the oil and separate the strands, drain, and they're ready to be stir-fried in a wok with the other ingredients. They're found in the refrigerated section at the supermarket.

600g hokkien noodles
600g lamb strips
2 tablespoons cornflour
1 teaspoon salt
¼ cup (60ml) peanut oil
1 medium brown onion (150g), sliced thickly
1 clove garlic, crushed
1cm piece fresh ginger (5g), grated
1 large red capsicum (350g), sliced thinly
200g snow peas, trimmed, halved
⅓ cup (80ml) plum sauce
¼ cup (60ml) oyster sauce
¼ cup (60ml) chicken stock
2 teaspoons tamarind concentrate

1. Place noodles in large heatproof bowl; cover with hot water, separate with fork, drain.
2. Place lamb in large bowl with cornflour and salt; toss lamb to coat in mixture. Heat 1 tablespoon of the oil in wok; stir-fry lamb, in batches, until browned all over.
3. Heat remaining oil in same wok; stir-fry onion, garlic and ginger until onion softens. Add capsicum and snow peas; stir-fry until just tender.
4. Return lamb to wok with noodles, sauces, stock and paste; stir-fry until heated through.

serves 4
per serving 28g total fat (8.5g saturated fat); 2817kJ (674 cal); 64.4g carbohydrate; 41.2g protein; 5.4g fibre

pepper-crusted fillet with penne in creamy red capsicum sauce

PREPARATION TIME 10 MINUTES **COOKING TIME** 25 MINUTES

3 medium red capsicums (600g)
600g lamb fillets
1 tablespoon cracked black pepper
1 tablespoon olive oil
1 medium brown onion (150g), chopped finely
2 cloves garlic, crushed
300ml cream
375g penne
⅔ cup coarsely chopped fresh basil

1. Quarter capsicums; discard seeds and membranes. Roast under grill or in very hot oven, skin-side up, until skin blisters and blackens. Cover capsicum pieces in plastic or paper 5 minutes; peel away skin then chop capsicum coarsely.
2. Place lamb and pepper in medium bowl; toss lamb to coat in pepper. Cook lamb, in batches, in heated large oiled frying pan until browned all over and cooked as desired. Cover lamb; stand 5 minutes then slice thinly.
3. Heat oil in same pan; cook onion and garlic, stirring, until onion softens. Add cream; bring to a boil. Remove from heat; blend or process cream mixture with capsicum until mixture is smooth.
4. Meanwhile, cook pasta in large saucepan of boiling water, uncovered, until just tender; drain.
5. Place pasta in large bowl with lamb, capsicum sauce and basil; toss gently.

serves 4
per serving 51.9g total fat (28.5g saturated fat); 3946kJ (944 cal); 73.3g carbohydrate; 46.3g protein; 6.1g fibre

One of the simplest but most delicious appetisers is a small plate of roasted capsicum drizzled with extra virgin olive oil and a smattering of salt and crushed garlic. Roasted capsicum are very different in taste from raw ones; the bitter taste of the skin is eliminated by peeling, and cooking the flesh brings out its lusciously sweet flavour.

mongolian lamb stir-fry

PREPARATION TIME 15 MINUTES **COOKING TIME** 20 MINUTES

The young edible shoots of various types of bamboo, pale yellow, crunchy and fibrous, are available fresh from Asian greengrocers and food shops as well as peeled, sliced, cooked and canned from supermarkets. Rinse the canned variety well to rid the shoots of all traces of the can liquid.

1½ cups (300g) white long-grain rice
2 tablespoons peanut oil
600g lamb strips
2 cloves garlic, crushed
1cm piece fresh ginger (5g), grated
1 medium brown onion (150g), sliced thickly
1 medium red capsicum (200g), sliced thickly
230g can bamboo shoots, rinsed, drained
¼ cup (60ml) soy sauce
1 tablespoon black bean sauce
1 tablespoon cornflour
2 tablespoons rice wine vinegar
6 green onions, cut into 5cm lengths

1. Cook rice in large saucepan of boiling water, uncovered, until just tender; drain. Cover to keep warm.
2. Meanwhile, heat half of the oil in wok; stir-fry lamb, in batches, until browned all over.
3. Heat remaining oil in same wok; stir-fry garlic, ginger and brown onion until onion softens. Add capsicum and bamboo shoots; stir-fry until vegetables are just tender. Return lamb to wok with sauces and blended cornflour and vinegar; stir-fry until sauce boils and thickens slightly. Remove from heat; stir in green onion. Serve stir-fry with rice.

serves 4
per serving 23.2g total fat (7.8g saturated fat); 2709kJ (648 cal); 68.7g carbohydrate; 40.4g protein; 3.5g fibre

WEEKENDS

These lamb cuts are just perfect for longer, slower cooking – the meat falls off the bones and melts in your mouth, making a perfect Sunday lunch.

scotch broth

PREPARATION TIME 30 MINUTES **COOKING TIME** 1 HOUR 40 MINUTES

Savoy cabbage is a large-headed, crimpled-leafed, loose-centred member of the same family as Brussels sprouts, cauliflower and broccoli. Less potent than other cabbages, it can be added to soups, stews and casseroles without fear of it overpowering the dish.

1kg neck chops
2.25 litres (9 cups) water
¾ cup (150g) pearl barley
1 large brown onion (200g), diced into 1cm pieces
2 medium carrots (240g), diced into 1cm pieces
1 medium leek (350g), sliced thinly
2 cups (160g) finely shredded savoy cabbage
½ cup (60g) frozen peas
2 tablespoons coarsely chopped fresh flat-leaf parsley

1 Combine chops with the water and barley in large saucepan; bring to a boil. Reduce heat; simmer, covered, 1 hour, skimming fat from surface occasionally. Add onion, carrot and leek; simmer, covered, about 30 minutes or until vegetables are tender.
2 Remove chops from soup mixture; when cool enough to handle, remove meat, chop coarsely. Discard bones.
3 Return meat to soup with cabbage and peas; cook, uncovered, about 10 minutes or until cabbage is tender. Sprinkle parsley over scotch broth just before serving.

serves 4
per serving 25.9g total fat (11.4g saturated fat); 2278kJ (545 cal); 32.6g carbohydrate; 45.6g protein; 10.3g fibre

cassoulet

PREPARATION TIME 40 MINUTES (PLUS STANDING TIME) **COOKING TIME** 1 HOUR 40 MINUTES

There are many regional variations of French cassoulet, and ours is based on a traditional Toulousaine version which traditionally calls for mutton.
We used dried white haricot beans in this recipe, but great northern, cannellini, navy or even lima beans can be used if you prefer.

1 Place beans in large bowl, cover with water; soak overnight, drain. Rinse under cold water; drain. Place beans in medium saucepan covered with boiling water; bring to a boil. Reduce heat; simmer, covered, about 15 minutes or until beans are just tender. Drain.
2 Preheat oven to moderately slow (160°C/140°C fan-forced).
3 Cook bacon in large flameproof casserole dish over high heat, pressing down with back of spoon, until browned all over; remove from dish. Cook sausage in same dish until browned all over; remove from dish.
4 Cook onion, celery and garlic in same dish, stirring, about 5 minutes or until soft. Add rosemary, bay leaves, undrained tomatoes, stock, beans, bacon and sausage; bring to a boil. Cover; cook in moderately slow oven 30 minutes. Remove from oven; sprinkle with combined breadcrumbs and parsley. Return to oven; cook, covered, 30 minutes. Uncover; cook about 10 minutes or until top browns lightly.
5 Meanwhile, make herb and rocket salad by combining rocket, parsley, chervil and basil in large bowl. Place remaining ingredients in screw-top jar; shake vinaigrette well.
6 Toss salad with vinaigrette just before serving with cassoulet.

serves 4
per serving 44.3g total fat (13.9g saturated fat); 3603kJ (862 cal); 58g carbohydrate; 57.3g protein; 15.1g fibre

1 cup (200g) dried white beans
150g piece streaky bacon, rind removed, diced into 1cm pieces
500g thin lamb sausages, sliced thickly
1 medium brown onion (150g), chopped finely
2 trimmed celery stalks (200g), chopped finely
2 cloves garlic, crushed
1 sprig fresh rosemary
2 bay leaves
425g can crushed tomatoes
1½ cups (375ml) chicken stock
2 cups (140g) stale breadcrumbs
⅓ cup coarsely chopped fresh flat-leaf parsley

HERB AND ROCKET SALAD
60g baby rocket leaves
1 cup loosely packed fresh flat-leaf parsley leaves
1 cup loosely packed fresh chervil sprigs
½ cup loosely packed fresh basil leaves
¼ cup (60ml) olive oil
2 tablespoons red wine vinegar
1 teaspoon white sugar

jerk mini roasts with black bean salad

PREPARATION TIME 30 MINUTES (PLUS STANDING AND REFRIGERATION TIME) **COOKING TIME** 40 MINUTES

1 cup (200g) dried black beans
2 mini roasts (700g)
¼ cup (60ml) olive oil
1 large brown onion (200g), chopped finely
1 clove garlic, crushed
1 long green chilli, chopped finely
1 teaspoon ground cumin
2 tablespoons red wine vinegar
1 large tomato (220g), seeded, chopped coarsely
½ cup firmly packed fresh coriander leaves
3 green onions, sliced thinly
2 tablespoons lime juice

JERK MARINADE
3 long green chillies, chopped finely
3 green onions, chopped finely
2 cloves garlic, crushed
1 teaspoon ground allspice
1 teaspoon dried thyme
1 teaspoon white sugar
1 tablespoon soy sauce
1 tablespoon lime juice

Jerk is a Jamaican spice blend used to marinate meat, seafood or poultry before grilling or roasting. While each cook has his or her particular favourite combination of spices, jerk always contains allspice, thyme and chilli.
Black beans, also known as turtle beans, are a common ingredient in Caribbean and Latin American soups, salsas and salads. They are not the same as chinese black beans, which are fermented soy beans. They are available from greengrocers and delicatessens.

1. Place beans in medium bowl, cover with water; soak overnight.
2. Combine ingredients for jerk marinade in large bowl; add lamb, rub all over with marinade. Cover; refrigerate overnight.
3. Preheat oven to moderate (180°C/160°C fan-forced).
4. Drain beans; rinse under cold water. Place drained beans in medium saucepan, cover with water; bring to a boil. Reduce heat; simmer, uncovered, about 20 minutes or until tender, drain.
5. Meanwhile, heat half of the oil in medium flameproof casserole dish; cook lamb, uncovered, until browned all over. Roast lamb, uncovered, in moderate oven about 20 minutes or until cooked as desired. Cover lamb; stand 10 minutes then slice thickly.
6. Meanwhile, heat remaining oil in same cleaned saucepan; cook brown onion, garlic, chilli and cumin, stirring, until onion softens. Add vinegar; cook, stirring, until liquid evaporates. Remove from heat.
7. Combine onion mixture, beans, tomato, coriander, green onion and juice in large bowl; toss gently. Serve salad with roast.

serves 4
per serving 30.2g total fat (9g saturated fat); 2353kJ (563 cal); 22.4g carbohydrate; 49.8g protein; 12.8g fibre

garlic and sage lamb racks

PREPARATION TIME 10 MINUTES **COOKING TIME** 25 MINUTES

1 Preheat oven to hot (220°C/200°C fan-forced).
2 Halve onions, slice into thin wedges; place in large baking dish with sage leaves and half of the oil.
3 Combine remaining oil in small bowl with chopped sage and garlic. Press sage mixture all over lamb; place on onion in dish.
4 Roast, uncovered, in hot oven about 25 minutes or until lamb is browned all over and cooked as desired. Cover lamb racks; stand 10 minutes.

tip Red onions are sweet and have a less aggressive flavour than their brown and white counterparts.

serves 4
per serving 31.3g fat (8.5g saturated fat); 1676kJ (401 cal); 12.4g carbohydrate; 18.4g protein; 3.4g fibre

3 large red onions (900g)

12 fresh sage leaves

⅓ cup (80ml) olive oil

2 tablespoons coarsely chopped fresh sage

4 cloves garlic, chopped coarsely

4 x 4 french-trimmed cutlet racks (600g)

harissa-marinated leg with warm couscous salad

PREPARATION TIME 40 MINUTES (PLUS STANDING AND REFRIGERATION TIME) **COOKING TIME** 1 HOUR 5 MINUTES

30g dried red chillies, chopped coarsely
1 teaspoon ground cumin
1 teaspoon ground coriander
1 teaspoon caraway seeds
2 cloves garlic, crushed
1 teaspoon salt
1 teaspoon white sugar
⅓ cup (90g) tomato puree
⅓ cup (80ml) olive oil
2kg lamb leg

WARM COUSCOUS SALAD
2 small kumara (500g), diced into 1cm pieces
cooking-oil spray
2 cups (400g) couscous
½ cup (60g) frozen peas, thawed
1 tablespoon finely grated lemon rind
2½ cups (625ml) boiling water
1 small red onion (100g), chopped finely
½ cup finely shredded fresh flat-leaf parsley
¼ cup finely shredded fresh mint
2 tablespoons olive oil
1 tablespoon red wine vinegar
¼ cup (60ml) lemon juice

Harissa, a traditional spice paste used throughout North Africa, is made from dried red chillies, garlic, olive oil and caraway seeds. It can be used as a rub for meat, an ingredient in sauces and dressings, or eaten on its own as a condiment.

1 Place chilli in small heatproof bowl, cover with boiling water; stand 1 hour. Drain chilli; reserve ¼ cup of the soaking liquid.
2 Dry-fry cumin, coriander and caraway in heated small frying pan until fragrant. Blend or process spices with chilli, reserved liquid, garlic, salt, sugar and tomato puree until mixture is almost smooth. With motor operating, add oil in thin, steady stream; process until harissa forms a smooth paste.
3 Reserve ⅓ cup harissa. Using sharp knife, pierce lamb all over; place in large bowl. Rub remaining harissa over lamb, pressing into cuts. Cover; refrigerate 3 hours or overnight.
4 Preheat oven to moderately hot (200°C/180°C fan-forced).
5 Pour enough water into large shallow baking dish to come about 5mm up the sides; place lamb on wire rack over dish. Roast, uncovered, in moderately hot oven about 1 hour or until cooked as desired. Cover lamb; stand 20 minutes then slice thinly.
6 Meanwhile, make warm couscous salad.
7 Serve lamb with salad.

WARM COUSCOUS SALAD Place kumara, in single layer, on oiled oven tray; coat with cooking-oil spray. Roast, uncovered, in moderately hot oven for last 30 minutes of lamb cooking time. Combine couscous, peas, rind and the water in large heatproof bowl; cover, stand about 5 minutes or until water is absorbed, fluffing with fork occasionally. Stir kumara, onion, herbs and combined olive oil, vinegar and juice into couscous salad just before serving.

serves 4
per serving 49g total fat (12.9g saturated fat); 5150kJ (1232 cal); 98.1g carbohydrate; 98.7g protein; 5.6g fibre

marinated leg with caponata and lemon thyme polenta

PREPARATION TIME 30 MINUTES (PLUS REFRIGERATIONTIME)
COOKING TIME 1 HOUR 45 MINUTES (PLUS STANDING TIME)

Caponata, a classic Sicilian eggplant and capsicum dish, is usually eaten at room temperature as part of an antipasti or as a relish accompanying a roast, as we suggest here.

1 Using sharp knife, pierce lamb all over; place in large bowl. Rub combined paprika, juice, oil and garlic all over lamb, pressing into cuts. Cover; refrigerate 3 hours or overnight.
2 Preheat oven to moderately hot (200°C/180°C fan-forced).
3 Pour stock into large shallow baking dish; place lamb on wire rack over dish, drizzle with any remaining paprika mixture. Roast, uncovered, in moderately hot oven 30 minutes, brushing lamb occasionally with pan juices. Reduce heat to moderate (180°C/160°C fan-forced); roast, uncovered, about 1 hour and 15 minutes or until lamb is cooked as desired. Cover lamb; stand 20 minutes.
4 Meanwhile, make caponata. Make lemon thyme polenta.
5 Serve sliced lamb, sprinkled with combined rind and thyme, with caponata and polenta.

CAPONATA Heat half of the oil in large saucepan; cook eggplant until browned all over. Remove from pan. Heat remaining oil in same pan; cook onion, stirring, until soft. Add garlic, celery and capsicum; cook, stirring, until vegetables soften. Stir in capers, vinegar, tomato, eggplant and half of the basil; cook, covered, over low heat about 15 minutes or until mixture thickens slightly. Stir remaining basil and pine nuts into caponata just before serving.

LEMON THYME POLENTA Combine the water and milk in large saucepan; bring to a boil. Gradually add polenta, stirring constantly. Reduce heat; cook, stirring, about 10 minutes or until polenta thickens. Stir in cheese and lemon thyme.

serves 4
per serving 52g total fat (17.7g saturated fat); 4544kJ (1087 cal); 52.3g carbohydrate; 102.7g protein; 8.5g fibre

2kg lamb leg
2 teaspoons sweet paprika
¼ cup (60ml) lemon juice
1 tablespoon olive oil
2 cloves garlic, crushed
3 cups (750ml) beef stock
2 teaspoons finely shredded lemon rind
2 tablespoons coarsely chopped fresh lemon thyme

CAPONATA
2 tablespoons olive oil
6 baby eggplants (360g), chopped coarsely
2 medium brown onions (300g), chopped coarsely
3 cloves garlic, crushed
2 trimmed celery stalks (200g), chopped coarsely
2 medium red capsicums (400g), chopped coarsely
1 tablespoon baby capers, rinsed, drained
2 tablespoons red wine vinegar
3 large egg tomatoes (270g), chopped coarsely
½ cup coarsely chopped fresh basil
¼ cup (40g) toasted pine nuts

LEMON THYME POLENTA
2 cups (500ml) water
2½ cups (625ml) milk
1 cup (170g) polenta
½ cup (40g) finely grated parmesan cheese
1 tablespoon fresh lemon thyme leaves

spice-crusted racks with potato wedges

PREPARATION TIME 15 MINUTES **COOKING TIME** 55 MINUTES

- 5 medium potatoes (1kg), cut into wedges
- ¼ cup (60ml) olive oil
- 4 x 4 french-trimmed cutlet racks (600g)
- ½ teaspoon dried chilli flakes
- 2 tablespoons kalonji seeds
- 2 tablespoons sesame seeds
- 1 clove garlic, crushed
- ½ cup loosely packed fresh flat-leaf parsley leaves

Kalonji, also known as nigella, are tiny, angular seeds, black on the outside and creamy within, having a sharp nutty flavour that can be enhanced by a brief toasting in a dry hot pan before use. Sprinkled over turkish bread or as an important spice in Indian cooking, kalonji can be found in most Asian and Middle-Eastern food shops.

1. Preheat oven to moderately hot (200°C/180°C fan-forced).
2. Combine potato and 2 tablespoons of the oil on oven tray. Cook potato, in single layer, uncovered, in moderately hot oven about 55 minutes or until browned lightly and crisp.
3. Meanwhile, place lamb on another oven tray; rub all over with combined remaining oil, chilli, seeds and garlic. Roast, uncovered, in moderately hot oven for about the last 20 minutes of potato cooking time or until browned and cooked as desired.
4. Toss parsley and potato in large bowl; serve with lamb and lemon wedges, if desired.

serves 4
per serving 31.6g total fat (8.4g saturated fat); 2044kJ (489 cal); 28.9g carbohydrate; 22.4g protein; 4.8g fibre

barbecued forequarter chops with three marinades

PREPARATION TIME 20 MINUTES (PLUS REFRIGERATION TIME) **COOKING TIME** 15 MINUTES

Make any or all of the three marinades shown here for your next family barbecue. Each recipe makes enough marinade for four forequarter chops (760g). Serve the grilled marinated chops with the green salad we suggest below.

green salad

1 lebanese cucumber (130g), chopped coarsely

90g mizuna

200g grape tomatoes, halved

3 green onions, sliced thinly

1 tablespoon finely chopped garlic chives

1 teaspoon finely grated orange rind

½ cup (125ml) orange juice

2 tablespoons lemon juice

2 cloves garlic, crushed

2 tablespoons olive oil

1 Combine cucumber, mizuna, tomato, onion and chives in large bowl. Combine rind, juices, garlic and oil in screw-top jar; shake well. Pour dressing over salad; toss gently to combine.

serves 4
per serving 9.4g total fat (1.3g saturated fat); 464kJ (111 cal); 5.5g carbohydrate; 1.2g protein; 2.2g fibre

mustard and balsamic

2 cloves garlic, crushed

½ cup (125ml) balsamic vinegar

1 tablespoon wholegrain mustard

2 tablespoons olive oil

1 Combine garlic, vinegar mustard and oil in large bowl; add chops, turn to coat in marinade. Cover; refrigerate 3 hours or overnight.
2 Cook drained lamb on heated oiled grill plate (or grill or barbecue) until browned both sides and cooked as desired.

serves 4
per serving (with chops)
22.5g total fat (7.7g saturated fat); 1409kJ (337 cal); 0.3g carbohydrate; 32.5g protein; 0.4g fibre

chilli and lemon grass

1 clove garlic, crushed

5cm stick (10g) finely chopped fresh lemon grass

1 teaspoon ground coriander

2 tablespoons fish sauce

1 fresh small red thai chilli, chopped finely

2 tablespoons peanut oil

1 Combine garlic, lemon grass, coriander, sauce, chilli and oil in large bowl; add chops, turn to coat in marinade. Cover; refrigerate 3 hours or overnight.
2 Cook drained lamb on heated oiled grill plate (or grill or barbecue) until browned both sides and cooked as desired.

serves 4
per serving (with chops)
22.4g total fat (8g saturated fat); 1400kJ (335 cal); 0.5g carbohydrate; 33g protein; 0.3g fibre

char sui and honey

¼ cup (60ml) char sui sauce

2 tablespoons honey

2 tablespoons vegetable oil

1 Combine char sui, honey and oil in large bowl; add chops, turn to coat in marinade. Cover; refrigerate 3 hours or overnight.
2 Cook drained lamb on heated oiled grill plate (or grill or barbecue), brushing with remaining oil, until browned both sides and cooked as desired.

serves 4
per serving (with chops)
23.3g total fat (7.7g saturated fat); 1697kJ (406 cal); 17.2g carbohydrate; 32.6g protein; 1.7g fibre

parmesan and gremolata racks with parsley and chilli risotto

PREPARATION TIME 30 MINUTES **COOKING TIME** 40 MINUTES

½ cup coarsely chopped fresh flat-leaf parsley

1 tablespoon finely grated lemon rind

⅓ cup (25g) finely grated parmesan cheese

3 cloves garlic, crushed

1 tablespoon olive oil

2 x 8 french-trimmed cutlet racks (600g)

PARSLEY AND CHILLI RISOTTO

3 cups (750ml) chicken stock

3 cups (750ml) water

1 tablespoon olive oil

1 medium brown onion (150g), chopped coarsely

1½ cups (300g) arborio rice

½ cup (125ml) dry white wine

1 teaspoon finely grated lemon rind

1 fresh small red thai chilli, chopped finely

½ cup (40g) finely grated parmesan cheese

2 cups loosely packed fresh flat-leaf parsley leaves

1 Preheat oven to moderately hot (200°C/180°C fan-forced).
2 Combine parsley, rind, cheese, garlic and oil in small bowl. Place lamb in large shallow oiled baking dish; press gremolata mixture onto fatty side of each rack. Roast, uncovered, in moderately hot oven about 30 minutes or until lamb is cooked as desired.
3 Meanwhile, make parsley and chilli risotto.
4 Cut each lamb rack in half. Serve with risotto.

PARSLEY AND CHILLI RISOTTO Combine stock and the water in medium saucepan; bring to a boil. Reduce heat; simmer, covered. Heat oil in large saucepan; cook onion, stirring, about 5 minutes or until onion softens. Add rice; stir to coat in mixture. Add wine; cook, stirring, until liquid is absorbed. Stir in 1 cup simmering stock mixture; cook, stirring, over low heat until liquid is absorbed. Continue adding stock mixture, in 1-cup batches, stirring, until liquid is almost absorbed after each addition. Total cooking time should be about 35 minutes or until rice is tender. Stir rind, chilli, cheese and parsley into risotto just before serving.

serves 4

per serving 28.5g total fat (11g saturated fat); 2713kJ (649 cal); 63.3g carbohydrate; 29.7g protein; 3.1g fibre

slow-roasted leg with artichokes and lemon

PREPARATION TIME 30 MINUTES **COOKING TIME** 4 HOURS

½ cup coarsely chopped fresh flat-leaf parsley
½ cup (75g) seeded kalamata olives, quartered
4 drained anchovy fillets
4 cloves garlic, quartered
2 teaspoons finely grated lemon rind
2 tablespoons lemon juice
2 tablespoons capers, rinsed, drained
2 tablespoons olive oil
2kg lamb leg
800g jerusalem artichokes (800g), halved lengthways
2 small red onions (200g), cut into wedges
2 medium lemons (280g), cut into wedges
12 cloves garlic, unpeeled

1. Preheat oven to slow (140°C/120°C fan-forced).
2. Blend or process parsley, olives, anchovies, quartered garlic, rind, juice, capers and 1 tablespoon of the oil until mixture is chopped coarsely.
3. Using sharp knife, pierce lamb down to the bone at 3cm intervals along the length of the leg. Spread olive mixture all over lamb, pressing into cuts.
4. Combine artichokes in large shallow baking dish with onion, lemon, unpeeled garlic and remaining oil.
5. Place lamb on artichoke mixture; cover tightly with foil. Roast in slow oven 4 hours. Serve lamb with vegetable mixture.

serves 4
per serving 30.4g total fat (10.4g saturated fat); 2888kJ (691 cal); 14.6g carbohydrate; 87.8g protein; 8.7g fibre

Looking like a knobbly parsnip, the jerusalem artichoke is a crisp tuber with the texture of a fresh water chestnut and its own unique earthy taste. It's a great winter vegetable, suiting casseroles, roasts and savoury pies, plus it makes a wonderful cream soup. After they're peeled, keep submerged in acidulated water to keep them from discolouring.

turkish herbed lamb pizza

PREPARATION TIME 45 MINUTES (PLUS STANDING TIME) **COOKING TIME** 35 MINUTES

- ¾ teaspoon dried yeast
- 1 teaspoon white sugar
- ¾ cup (180ml) warm water
- 2 cups (300g) plain flour
- 1 teaspoon salt
- cooking-oil spray
- 600g lamb mince
- 1 tablespoon olive oil
- 1 small brown onion (80g), chopped finely
- 1 clove garlic, crushed
- ½ teaspoon ground cinnamon
- 1½ teaspoons ground allspice
- ¼ cup (40g) pine nuts, chopped coarsely
- ¼ cup (70g) tomato paste
- 2 medium tomatoes (300g), seeded, chopped finely
- 1 cup (250ml) chicken stock
- 2 tablespoons lemon juice
- ¼ cup finely chopped fresh flat-leaf parsley
- ¼ cup finely chopped fresh mint
- ½ cup (140g) greek-style yogurt
- 2 tablespoons cold water

1. Whisk yeast, sugar and the warm water in small bowl; cover, stand in warm place about 15 minutes or until mixture is frothy.
2. Combine flour and salt in large bowl; stir in yeast mixture, mix to a soft dough. Knead on lightly floured surface about 10 minutes or until smooth and elastic. Place in large oiled bowl, turning dough once to coat in oil. Cover dough; stand in warm place about 1 hour or until dough is doubled in size.
3. Halve dough; knead each portion until smooth then roll out to oval shape measuring approximately 12cm x 35cm. Place each oval on a lightly oiled oven tray; spray lightly with cooking-oil spray. Cover; stand in warm place 30 minutes.
4. Preheat oven to very hot (240°C/220°C fan-forced).
5. Cook mince in heated large non-stick frying pan, stirring, until cooked through; place in medium bowl.
6. Heat oil in same pan; cook onion and garlic, stirring, until onion softens. Add spices and nuts; cook, stirring, about 5 minutes or until nuts are just toasted. Return mince to pan with tomato paste, tomato, stock and juice; cook, stirring, about 5 minutes or until liquid is almost evaporated. Remove pan from heat; stir in herbs.
7. Spoon mince mixture over pizza bases; cook, uncovered, in very hot oven about 15 minutes or until bases are cooked through and tops are browned lightly. Serve drizzled with combined yogurt and the cold water.

serves 4
per serving 26.5g total fat (7.7g saturated fat); 2805kJ (671 cal); 63g carbohydrate; 44.2g protein; 5.3g fibre

honey dijon racks with potato and kumara gratin

PREPARATION TIME 40 MINUTES (PLUS REFRIGERATION TIME) **COOKING TIME** 1 HOUR 10 MINUTES

1 Combine oil, mustard, vinegar, garlic and honey in large bowl; add lamb, turn to coat all over in marinade. Cover; refrigerate 3 hours or overnight.
2 Preheat oven to moderately hot (200°C/180°C fan-forced). Grease deep 19cm-square cake pan.
3 Using V-slicer, mandoline or sharp knife, cut kumara and potatoes into 2mm-thick slices; place half of the kumara slices, overlapping slightly, in prepared pan. Top with a layer using half of the potato, overlapping slices slightly. Repeat layering with remaining kumara and potato.
4 Blend flour with a little of the cream in medium jug to form a smooth paste; stir in remaining cream and milk. Pour cream mixture over potato and kumara. Cover gratin with foil; cook in moderately hot oven about 45 minutes or until vegetables are tender. Uncover gratin; sprinkle with cheese. Cook, uncovered, in moderately hot oven about 15 minutes or until cheese browns lightly. Stand gratin 5 minutes before serving.
5 Meanwhile, drain lamb; reserve marinade. Place lamb on wire rack in large shallow baking dish; cook, uncovered, in moderately hot oven for about the last 35 minutes of gratin cooking time or until cooked as desired. Cover to keep warm.
6 Bring reserved marinade to a boil in small saucepan. Reduce heat; simmer sauce, uncovered, 5 minutes. Serve gratin with lamb, drizzled with sauce.

serves 4
per serving 66.5g total fat (36.2g saturated fat); 3632kJ (869 cal); 42g carbohydrate; 27.6g protein; 3.4g fibre

2 tablespoons olive oil
2 teaspoons dijon mustard
¼ cup (60ml) red wine vinegar
2 cloves garlic, crushed
2 tablespoons honey
4 x 4 french-trimmed cutlet racks (600g)
1 medium kumara (400g)
2 medium potatoes (400g)
1 tablespoon plain flour
1¾ cups (430ml) cream
¼ cup (60ml) milk
¾ cup (75g) grated pizza cheese

chilli and honey-glazed loin with mee goreng

PREPARATION TIME 20 MINUTES COOKING TIME 45 MINUTES

Also sold as dried chinese mushrooms, the dried shiitake has a far more intense flavour than the fresh mushroom. Dried shiitake mushrooms need to be stored airtight in a dark, cool place then washed and soaked before use. Having an earthy intense flavour of their own, they also absorb the various flavours of the different ingredients with which they are cooked.

800g loin (boned and rolled)
1 tablespoon sambal oelek
1 tablespoon honey
1 tablespoon kecap manis

MEE GORENG
10 dried shiitake mushrooms
450g hokkien noodles
2 teaspoons peanut oil
1cm piece fresh ginger (5g), grated
1 clove garlic, crushed
1 green onion, sliced thinly
100g snow peas, sliced thinly
1 teaspoon sambal oelek
2 tablespoons kecap manis
1 tablespoon hoisin sauce
1 tablespoon oyster sauce
⅓ cup (80ml) beef stock

1 Preheat oven to moderate (180°C/160°C fan-forced).
2 Place lamb on wire rack over baking dish; brush with combined remaining ingredients. Roast lamb, uncovered, in moderate oven 30 minutes. Cover lamb; roast about 15 minutes or until cooked as desired. Cover lamb; stand 10 minutes.
3 Meanwhile, make mee goreng. Serve with sliced lamb.

MEE GORENG Place mushrooms in small heatproof bowl, cover with boiling water; stand 20 minutes or until tender, drain. Slice mushrooms thinly. Place noodles in large heatproof bowl; cover with boiling water, separate with fork, drain. Heat oil in wok; stir-fry ginger and garlic until fragrant. Add mushrooms and noodles to wok; stir-fry 2 minutes. Add remaining ingredients; stir-fry until snow peas are just tender.

serves 4
per serving 21.5g total fat (9.1g saturated fat); 2926kJ (700 cal); 70.2g carbohydrate; 55.4g protein; 3.6g fibre

duxelles-filled leg with roasted vegetables

PREPARATION TIME 30 MINUTES **COOKING TIME** 1 HOUR 45 MINUTES

A duxelles (doo-zell) is a classic French mixture of finely chopped mushrooms and shallots cooked in butter. It is used as an ingredient in the making of pâtés, sauces and stuffings.

- 40g butter
- 150g swiss brown mushrooms, chopped finely
- 1 clove garlic, crushed
- 3 shallots (75g), chopped finely
- ½ cup (125ml) balsamic vinegar
- 1.2kg easy carve lamb leg
- 1 teaspoon sea salt
- 2 large parsnips (700g)
- 2 large carrots (360g)
- 1 large kumara (500g)
- 2 large potatoes (600g)
- 2 tablespoons olive oil
- ½ cup (125ml) beef stock

1. Melt butter in large frying pan; cook mushrooms, garlic and shallot, stirring, until onion softens. Add half of the vinegar; bring to a boil. Reduce heat; simmer duxelles, uncovered, about 5 minutes or until liquid has evaporated.
2. Fill lamb cavity with duxelles; rub lamb all over with salt.
3. Preheat oven to moderate (180°C/160°C fan-forced).
4. Halve parsnips, carrots and kumara first crossways, then lengthways; cut pieces into thick slices. Cut potatoes into wedges. Place vegetables, in single layer, in large shallow flameproof baking dish; drizzle with oil. Place lamb on wire rack over vegetables; roast, uncovered, in moderate oven about 1 hour 30 minutes or until lamb is cooked as desired and vegetables are tender. Remove lamb and vegetables from dish, cover lamb; stand 10 minutes.
5. Meanwhile, place dish containing juices over heat; stir in stock and remaining vinegar, bring to a boil. Strain sauce into small jug. Serve vegetables with sliced lamb, drizzled with sauce.

serves 4
per serving 34.3g total fat (13.9g saturated fat); 3432kJ (821 cal); 50.5g carbohydrate; 76.5g protein; 11g fibre

greek roast lamb with skordalia and lemon-scented potatoes

PREPARATION TIME 40 MINUTES (PLUS REFRIGERATION TIME) **COOKING TIME** 4 HOURS 20 MINUTES

- 2kg lamb leg
- 2 cloves garlic, crushed
- ½ cup (125ml) lemon juice
- 2 tablespoons olive oil
- 1 tablespoon fresh oregano leaves
- 1 teaspoon fresh lemon thyme leaves
- 5 large potatoes (1.5kg), diced into 3cm pieces
- 2 tablespoons olive oil, extra
- 1 tablespoon finely grated lemon rind
- 2 tablespoons lemon juice
- 1 teaspoon fresh lemon thyme leaves

SKORDALIA

- 1 medium potato (200g), quartered
- 3 cloves garlic, quartered
- 1 tablespoon lemon juice
- 1 tablespoon white wine vinegar
- 2 tablespoons water
- ⅓ cup (80ml) olive oil
- 1 tablespoon warm water

Skordalia is a classic Greek accompaniment to meat, made from either potato or bread pureed with a large amount of garlic plus olive oil, lemon juice or vinegar, herbs and, occasionally, ground nuts.

1. Combine lamb with garlic, juice, oil, oregano and thyme in large bowl. Cover; refrigerate 3 hours or overnight.
2. Preheat oven to moderately slow (160°C/140°C fan-forced).
3. Place lamb in large baking dish; roast, uncovered, in moderately slow oven 4 hours.
4. Meanwhile, make skordalia.
5. Toss potato in large bowl with combined remaining ingredients; place, in single layer, on oven tray. Cook potato, uncovered, in moderately slow oven for last 30 minutes of lamb cooking time.
6. Remove lamb from oven; cover to keep warm.
7. Increase oven temperature to hot (220°C/200°C fan-forced); roast potatoes, uncovered, about 20 minutes or until crisp and tender. Serve potatoes and lamb with skordalia; sprinkle with extra fresh lemon thyme leaves, if desired.

SKORDALIA Boil, steam or microwave potato until tender; drain. Push potato through food mill or fine sieve into large bowl; cool 10 minutes. Place garlic, juice, vinegar and the water in bowl with potato; stir until well combined. Place potato mixture in blender; with motor operating, gradually add oil in a thin, steady stream, blending only until skordalia thickens (do not overmix). Stir in the water.

serves 4

per serving 57g total fat (14g saturated fat); 4556kJ (1090 cal); 51.5g carbohydrate; 91.2g protein; 6.7g fibre

barbecued loin chops with creamy mash and flavoured butter

PREPARATION TIME 25 MINUTES **COOKING TIME** 30 MINUTES

Make any one of the following three flavoured butter accompaniments to melt on your chops and serve with our yummy mashed potatoes.

4 large potatoes (1.2kg), chopped coarsely

50g butter

½ cup (120g) sour cream

8 loin chops (800g)

1 Make the flavoured butter of your choice (opposite).
2 Meanwhile, boil, steam or microwave potato until tender; drain. Mash potato in large bowl with butter and sour cream until smooth; cover to keep warm.
3 Cook lamb on heated oiled grill plate (or grill or barbecue) until browned both sides and cooked as desired. Serve lamb with mash and your chosen butter.

serves 4
per serving (without butter)
35.5g total fat
(20.9g saturated fat);
2587kJ (619 cal);
35.4g carbohydrate;
38.8g protein; 4.2g fibre

parsley and rosemary

1 tablespoon finely chopped fresh flat-leaf parsley

2 tablespoons finely chopped fresh rosemary

80g butter, softened

1 Blend or process ingredients until smooth. Place on piece of plastic wrap; shape into a rectangular block.
2 Wrap butter mixture tightly in plastic wrap. Freeze until just firm; remove 10 minutes before serving.

per serving (butter only)
16.4g total fat
(10.8g saturated fat);
610kJ (146 cal);
0.2g carbohydrate;
0.1g protein; 0.1g fibre

roast garlic and chilli

6 cloves garlic, unpeeled

1 fresh small red thai chilli, chopped finely

80g butter, softened

1 Preheat oven to moderately hot (200°C/180°C fan-forced).
2 Roast garlic in small baking dish, uncovered, in moderately hot oven about 15 minutes or until garlic is tender.
3 When cool enough to handle, peel garlic. Blend or process garlic, chilli and butter until smooth. Place on piece of plastic wrap; shape into a rectangular block.
4 Wrap butter mixture tightly in plastic wrap. Freeze until just firm; remove 10 minutes before serving.

per serving (butter only)
16.5g total fat
(10.8g saturated fat);
627kJ (150 cal);
0.2g carbohydrate;
0.4g protein; 0.8g fibre

lemon and pepper

2 teaspoons finely grated lemon rind

1 tablespoon lemon juice

1 tablespoon cracked black pepper

80g butter, softened

1 Blend or process ingredients until smooth. Place on piece of plastic wrap; shape into a rectangular block.
2 Wrap butter mixture tightly in plastic wrap. Freeze until just firm; remove 10 minutes before serving.

per serving (butter only)
16.5g total fat
(10.8g saturated fat);
635kJ (150 cal);
0.9g carbohydrate;
0.3g protein; 0.5g fibre

doner kebab

PREPARATION TIME 25 MINUTES (PLUS REFRIGERATION TIME) **COOKING TIME** 10 MINUTES

Baharat, a spice mix used in countries surrounding the Persian Gulf, can be made of any of an array of pungent spices, among them paprika, chilli, black pepper, cinnamon, clove, nutmeg, allspice, coriander and cumin. Make a simple version by grinding together a quarter cup each of black peppercorns and allspice, 2 teaspoons of ground cinnamon and 1 of nutmeg.

4 cloves garlic, crushed
1 teaspoon baharat
¼ cup (60ml) olive oil
2 tablespoons lemon juice
600g butterflied steaks
2 cloves garlic, crushed, extra
⅓ cup (95g) greek-style yogurt
½ cup (130g) hummus
4 large pitta
1 baby cos lettuce, shredded finely
3 large egg tomatoes (270g), seeded, chopped coarsely

1. Combine garlic, baharat, 2 tablespoons of the oil and 1 tablespoon of the juice in large bowl; add steaks, turn to coat in mixture. Cover; refrigerate 3 hours or overnight.
2. Meanwhile, combine remaining oil, remaining juice, extra garlic and yogurt in small jug, cover; refrigerate until required.
3. Cook steaks on heated oiled grill plate (or grill or barbecue) until browned both sides and cooked as desired. Slice thinly.
4. Spread hummus evenly over each pitta; divide lettuce, tomato and steak among pitta, drizzle with yogurt sauce. Roll pitta tightly to completely enclose filling.

serves 4
per serving 36g total fat (10.7g saturated fat); 2884kJ (690 cal); 46.9g carbohydrate; 44.4g protein; 7.1g fibre

lamb wrapped in banana leaf with thai salad

PREPARATION TIME 50 MINUTES (PLUS REFRIGERATION TIME) **COOKING TIME** 25 MINUTES

1 cup coarsely chopped fresh coriander

2 coriander roots, chopped finely

10cm stick (20g) finely chopped fresh lemon grass

2 cloves garlic, crushed

1 teaspoon finely grated lime rind

2 tablespoons lime juice

1 fresh small red thai chilli, chopped finely

1 tablespoon grated palm sugar

2 tablespoons fish sauce

2 mini roasts (700g)

2 large banana leaves

cooking-oil spray

THAI SALAD

2 medium carrots (240g), cut into matchsticks

150g snow peas, trimmed, sliced thinly

4 green onions, sliced thinly

½ cup coarsely chopped fresh coriander

½ cup coarsely chopped fresh mint

1 medium red capsicum (200g), sliced thinly

1 shallot (25g), sliced thinly

1. Combine chopped fresh coriander, coriander root, lemon grass, garlic, juice, rind, chilli, sugar and sauce in large bowl; add lamb, turn to coat in marinade. Cover; refrigerate 3 hours or overnight.
2. Preheat oven to moderate (180°C/160°C fan-forced).
3. Strain lamb through fine sieve over medium bowl; reserve marinade solids in strainer and marinade in separate bowl for thai salad. Cut each lamb roast in half horizontally.
4. Trim banana leaves into four 30cm squares. Using tongs, dip one square at a time into large saucepan of boiling water, remove immediately. Rinse under cold water; pat dry with absorbent paper. Banana leaf squares should be soft and pliable.
5. Using fingers, press lamb halves all over with marinade solids; place each half in the centre of one of the banana leaf squares. Fold banana leaf over lamb to enclose; secure each parcel with kitchen string.
6. Place lamb parcels, in single layer, in large shallow baking dish; spray parcels with cooking-oil spray. Cook, uncovered, in moderate oven about 30 minutes or until roast is cooked as desired.
7. Meanwhile, make thai salad. Serve lamb on opened banana leaf with salad.

THAI SALAD Combine ingredients in large bowl. Place remaining reserved marinade in small saucepan; bring to a boil. Reduce heat; simmer, uncovered, 2 minutes. Cool marinade 10 minutes, pour over salad; toss gently.

tip Banana leaves can be ordered from greengrocers.

serves 4
per serving 16.6g total fat (7.1g saturated fat); 1488kJ (356 cal); 11.1g carbohydrate; 40.5g protein; 4.9g fibre

shanks in five-spice, tamarind and ginger

PREPARATION TIME 20 MINUTES COOKING TIME 2 HOURS 10 MINUTES

Small, fresh and plump sugar snap peas, also known as honey snap peas, are eaten whole, pod and all, similarly to snow peas. They are just as good tossed raw in a salad as they are, as we suggest here, boiled, steamed or microwaved, either alone or with complementary vegetables, and eaten as an accompaniment to a substantial main course.

2 teaspoons five-spice powder
1 teaspoon dried chilli flakes
1 cinnamon stick
2 star anise
¼ cup (60ml) soy sauce
½ cup (125ml) chinese rice wine
2 tablespoons tamarind concentrate
2 tablespoons brown sugar
8cm piece fresh ginger (40g), grated
2 cloves garlic, chopped coarsely
1¼ cups (310ml) water
8 french-trimmed shanks (1.6kg)
500g choy sum, chopped into 10cm lengths
150g sugar snap peas, trimmed

1. Preheat oven to moderate (180°C/160°C fan-forced).
2. Cook five-spice, chilli, cinnamon and star anise in small frying pan, stirring, until fragrant. Combine spices with soy, wine, tamarind, sugar, ginger, garlic and the water in medium jug.
3. Place shanks, in single layer, in large shallow baking dish; drizzle with spice mixture. Roast, uncovered, in moderate oven, turning shanks occasionally, about 2 hours or until meat is almost falling off the shanks. Remove shanks from dish; cover to keep warm. Skim away excess fat; strain sauce into small saucepan.
4. Meanwhile, boil, steam or microwave choy sum and peas, separately, until tender; drain.
5. Divide vegetables among serving plates; serve with shanks, drizzled with reheated sauce.

serves 4

per serving 20g total fat (9g saturated fat); 1885kJ (451 cal); 12.5g carbohydrate; 48.3g protein; 3.1g fibre

tandoori with dhal, raita and pickled lemon

PREPARATION TIME 1 HOUR (PLUS REFRIGERATION TIME)
COOKING TIME 2 HOURS

2 x 700g butterflied shoulders
2 large eggplants (1kg), cut lengthways into eight wedges
2 large pieces naan

TANDOORI PASTE
2 teaspoons cumin seeds
2 teaspoons coriander seeds
1 teaspoon cardamom seeds
2 teaspoons garam masala
1 teaspoon salt
1 teaspoon cracked black pepper
3 cloves garlic, crushed
2cm piece fresh ginger (10g), chopped coarsely
1 fresh long red chilli, quartered
3 green onions, chopped coarsely
¼ cup (60ml) lemon juice
½ cup firmly packed fresh coriander leaves
1 cup (280g) yogurt

DHAL
20g butter
3 cloves garlic, crushed
1 large brown onion (200g), chopped finely
1 teaspoon ground cumin
1 teaspoon garam masala
4 curry leaves
1 cup (200g) yellow split peas
3 cups (750ml) water

RAITA
¼ cup finely chopped fresh mint
¼ cup finely chopped fresh coriander
1 cup (280g) yogurt
1 clove garlic, crushed
2cm piece fresh ginger (10g), chopped finely
1 tablespoon lemon juice

PICKLED LEMON
1 tablespoon vegetable oil
2 teaspoons yellow mustard seeds
4 curry leaves
¼ cup (60ml) white wine vinegar
2 medium lemons (280g), chopped coarsely

1. Make tandoori paste; reserve two tablespoons in small bowl. Combine lamb with remaining paste in large bowl; turn to coat all over in paste. Cover; refrigerate 1 hour.
2. Meanwhile, make dhal. Make raita. Make pickled lemon.
3. Preheat oven to moderate (180°C/160°C fan-forced). Cook lamb on heated oiled grill (or grill plate or barbecue) about 20 minutes or until browned all over. Place lamb in shallow baking dish; roast, uncovered, in moderate oven about 35 minutes or until cooked as desired. Cover lamb; stand 15 minutes then slice thickly.
4. Meanwhile, cook eggplant on same heated oiled grill (or grill plate or barbecue), brushing with reserved tandoori paste, about 10 minutes or until eggplant is tender. Cover; stand 10 minutes.
5. Toast naan both sides on heated oiled grill.
6. Serve lamb with eggplant, dhal, raita, pickled lemon and naan.

TANDOORI PASTE Cook seeds in heated dry medium frying pan, stirring, until fragrant. Blend or process seeds with remaining ingredients until smooth.

DHAL Heat butter in medium saucepan; cook garlic and onion, stirring, until onion softens. Add spices; cook, stirring, until fragrant. Add curry leaves, split peas and the water; bring to a boil. Reduce heat; simmer, uncovered, about 45 minutes or until split peas are tender.

RAITA Combine ingredients in medium bowl.

PICKLED LEMON Heat oil in medium frying pan; fry seeds, stirring, until they begin to pop. Add curry leaves, vinegar and lemon; cook until heated through. Drain; discard any excess liquid.

serves 6
per serving 59.2g total fat (24.2g saturated fat); 5238kJ (1253 cal); 100g carbohydrate; 81.6g protein; 11.4g fibre

cardamom-crumbed cutlets with risotto milanese

PREPARATION TIME 15 MINUTES COOKING TIME 40 MINUTES

¼ cup (35g) plain flour
1 egg
1 cup (70g) stale breadcrumbs
1 teaspoon finely grated lemon rind
1 tablespoon ground cardamom
½ cup finely chopped fresh flat-leaf parsley
16 french-trimmed cutlets (800g)
3 cups (750ml) chicken stock
2 cups (500ml) water
2 tablespoons olive oil
1 clove garlic, crushed
1 medium brown onion (150g), chopped coarsely
1¼ cups (250g) arborio rice
pinch saffron threads
¼ cup (60ml) dry white wine
100g baby spinach leaves
20g butter
¼ cup (60ml) olive oil extra

1 Place flour in small shallow bowl; whisk egg in separate small shallow bowl. Combine breadcrumbs, rind, cardamom and parsley in separate medium shallow bowl. Coat cutlets, one at a time, in flour then egg then breadcrumb mixture. Place cutlets, in single layer, on tray, cover; refrigerate until required.
2 Bring stock and the water to a boil in medium saucepan. Reduce heat; simmer, covered. Heat oil in large saucepan; cook garlic and onion, stirring, until onion softens. Add rice and saffron; stir rice to coat in mixture. Add wine; bring to a boil. Reduce heat; simmer, stirring, 2 minutes. Stir in 1 cup of the simmering stock mixture; cook, stirring, over low heat, until liquid is absorbed. Continue adding stock mixture, in 1-cup batches, stirring until liquid is absorbed after each addition. Total cooking time should be about 35 minutes or until rice is just tender. Stir spinach and butter into risotto just before serving.
3 When risotto is almost cooked, heat extra oil in large frying pan; cook cutlets, in batches, until browned both sides and cooked as desired. Serve cutlets with risotto.

serves 4
per serving 47.2g total fat (14.7g saturated fat); 3536kJ (846 cal); 71g carbohydrate; 32.7g protein; 3.2g fibre

navarin of lamb

PREPARATION TIME 30 MINUTES **COOKING TIME** 1 HOUR 15 MINUTES

Rather like a French version of a hot pot, a navarin is an aromatic stew, which, in the spring, is traditionally made with the best of new season vegetables and lamb.

2 tablespoons olive oil
8 chump chops (880g)
1 medium brown onion (150g), sliced thinly
3 cloves garlic, crushed
2 tablespoons plain flour
2 cups (500ml) vegetable stock
2 cups (500ml) water
2 x 400g cans diced tomatoes
½ teaspoon black peppercorns
2 bay leaves
1 sprig fresh rosemary
8 baby new potatoes (320g), halved
3 small brown onions (240g), quartered
1 bunch baby turnips (500g), trimmed, peeled, quartered
10 baby carrots (200g), halved lengthways
1 cup (120g) frozen peas
½ cup coarsely chopped fresh flat-leaf parsley

1 Heat oil in large heavy-based saucepan; cook chops, in batches, only until browned.
2 Cook sliced onion in same pan, stirring, until just softened. Add garlic and flour; stir until mixture bubbles and thickens. Gradually add stock and the water; stir until mixture boils and thickens slightly. Return chops to pan with undrained tomatoes, peppercorns, bay leaves and rosemary; bring to a boil. Reduce heat; simmer, covered, 20 minutes.
3 Add potato, quartered onion, turnip and carrot to pan; simmer, covered, 30 minutes, stirring occasionally. Add peas; simmer, uncovered, until peas are just tender. Sprinkle parsley over navarin just before serving.

serves 4
per serving 37.2g total fat (13.7g saturated fat); 2721kJ (651 cal); 35.5g carbohydrate; 43.3g protein; 11.9g fibre

It's true that rosemary is for remembrance... and it's also for the distinctively pungent flavour of lemon and pine that it imparts to food. Grown throughout the southern Mediterranean, it's used in many of the hearty stews and casseroles of Provence and northern Italy. Rosemary's robust taste offers a foil to the richness of roast lamb, pork and game, and it helps enliven the bland doughiness of plain breads, biscuits and dumplings.

moussaka

PREPARATION TIME 40 MINUTES (PLUS STANDING TIME) COOKING TIME 1 HOUR 30 MINUTES

2 large eggplants (1kg), sliced thinly

1 tablespoon coarse cooking salt

¼ cup (60ml) olive oil

1 large brown onion (200g), chopped finely

2 cloves garlic, crushed

1kg lamb mince

425g can crushed tomatoes

½ cup (125ml) dry white wine

1 teaspoon ground cinnamon

¼ cup (20g) finely grated parmesan cheese

WHITE SAUCE

80g butter

⅓ cup (50g) plain flour

2 cups (500ml) milk

1 Place eggplant in colander, sprinkle all over with salt; stand 30 minutes. Rinse under cold water; drain. Pat dry with absorbent paper.
2 Heat oil in large frying pan; cook eggplant, in batches, until browned both sides; drain on absorbent paper.
3 Cook onion and garlic in same pan, stirring, until onion softens. Add mince; cook, stirring, until mince changes colour. Stir in undrained tomatoes, wine and cinnamon; bring to a boil. Reduce heat; simmer, uncovered, about 30 minutes or until liquid has evaporated.
4 Meanwhile, preheat oven to moderate (180°C/160°C fan-forced). Oil shallow 2-litre (8-cup) rectangular baking dish.
5 Make white sauce.
6 Place a third of the eggplant, overlapping slices slightly, in prepared dish; spread half of the meat sauce over eggplant. Repeat layering with another third of the eggplant, remaining meat sauce and remaining eggplant. Spread white sauce over top layer of eggplant; sprinkle with cheese. Cook, uncovered, in moderate oven about 40 minutes or until top browns lightly. Cover moussaka; stand 10 minutes before serving.

WHITE SAUCE Melt butter in medium saucepan. Add flour; cook, stirring, until mixture thickens and bubbles. Gradually add milk; stir until mixture boils and thickens.

serves 6
per serving 36.6g total fat (16.5g saturated fat); 2420kJ (579 cal); 18g carbohydrate; 41.8g protein; 5.3g fibre

barbecued steaks and vegetable chips with chutney

PREPARATION TIME 45 MINUTES **COOKING TIME** UP TO 1 HOUR 5 MINUTES

Make any one of the following three chutneys to accompany your steaks and chips.

8 butterflied steaks (720g)

1 large kumara (500g), sliced thinly

2 large parsnips (700g), sliced thinly

1 Make the chutney of your choice (opposite).
2 Meanwhile, cook steaks, kumara and parsnips, in batches, on heated oiled grill plate (or grill or barbecue) until browned both sides and cooked as desired.
3 Serve lamb and chips with your chosen chutney.

serves 4
per serving (without chutney)
16.3g total fat
(7.2g saturated fat);
1835kJ (439 cal);
30.6g carbohydrate;
42.4g protein; 5.8g fibre

tamarind and date

1 teaspoon ground cumin

½ teaspoon dried chilli flakes

⅓ cup (80ml) tamarind concentrate

1 cup (160g) coarsely chopped seeded dates

½ cup (110g) firmly packed brown sugar

4cm piece fresh ginger (20g), coarsely grated

½ cup (125ml) water

1 Dry-fry cumin and chilli in heated medium saucepan, stirring, until fragrant. Add remaining ingredients; bring to a boil. Reduce heat; simmer, uncovered, stirring occasionally, about 5 minutes or until thick.

makes 1 cup
per ¼-cup serving (chutney only) 0.1g total fat (0g saturated fat); 698kJ (167 cal); 42.7g carbohydrate; 0.7g protein; 2.3g fibre

rhubarb and apple

1 teaspoon vegetable oil

1 medium brown onion (150g), chopped coarsely

4 cups (440g) coarsely chopped rhubarb

2 medium green apples (300g), chopped coarsely

½ cup (125ml) red wine vinegar

½ cup (125ml) orange juice

¾ cup (165g) caster sugar

1 cinnamon stick

½ cup (80g) sultanas

1 Heat oil in large saucepan; cook onion, stirring, until soft. Add remaining ingredients; bring to a boil, stirring. Reduce heat; simmer, uncovered, stirring occasionally, about 1 hour or until chutney thickens.

tip You need approximately seven large rhubarb stalks for this recipe.

makes 2 cups
per ¼-cup serving (chutney only) 0.8g total fat (0.1g saturated fat); 627kJ (150 cal); 34.6g carbohydrate; 1.6g protein; 3g fibre

tomato and chilli

4 large tomatoes (880g), peeled, chopped coarsely

1 medium brown onion (150g), chopped coarsely

½ cup (110g) firmly packed brown sugar

1 cup (250ml) white wine vinegar

1 tablespoon ground ginger

1 medium green apple (150g), chopped coarsely

½ cup (85g) raisins

1 teaspoon dried chilli flakes

1 teaspoon cracked black pepper

2 tablespoons tomato paste

1 Combine ingredients in large saucepan; bring to a boil, stirring. Reduce heat, simmer, uncovered, stirring occasionally, about 1 hour or until chutney thickens.

makes 2 cups
per ¼-cup serving (chutney only) 0.2g total fat (0g saturated fat); 481kJ (115 cal); 25.9g carbohydrate; 1.8g protein; 2.5g fibre

lamb and quince tagine with pistachio couscous

PREPARATION TIME 20 MINUTES **COOKING TIME** 1 HOUR 30 MINUTES

As with the word casserole, tagine also has two different culinary meanings. Originally from Moroccan kitchens and now found in many of ours, a tagine is the earthenware, cone-lidded vessel in which the spicy, fragrant North African stew with the same name is cooked. The lid serves as a vent, allowing the steam to escape, thus concentrating the flavours of the food inside.

40g butter
600g diced lamb
1 medium red onion (170g), chopped coarsely
2 cloves garlic, crushed
1 cinnamon stick
2 teaspoons ground coriander
1 teaspoon ground cumin
1 teaspoon ground ginger
1 teaspoon dried chilli flakes
1½ cups (375ml) water
425g can crushed tomatoes
2 medium quinces (600g), quartered
1 large green zucchini (150g), chopped coarsely
2 tablespoons coarsely chopped fresh coriander

PISTACHIO COUSCOUS
1½ cups (300g) couscous
1 cup (250ml) boiling water
20g butter, softened
½ cup finely chopped fresh coriander
¼ cup (35g) toasted shelled pistachios, chopped coarsely

1 Melt butter in large saucepan; cook lamb, in batches, until browned. Add onion to same pan; cook, stirring, until softened. Add garlic, cinnamon, ground coriander, cumin, ginger and chilli; cook, stirring, until mixture is fragrant.
2 Return lamb to pan. Stir in the water, undrained tomatoes and quince; bring to a boil. Reduce heat; simmer, covered, 30 minutes. Uncover; simmer, stirring occasionally, about 1 hour or until quince is tender and sauce has thickened.
3 Add zucchini; cook, stirring, about 10 minutes or until zucchini is just tender. Meanwhile, make couscous.
4 Serve couscous with tagine, sprinkled with coriander.

PISTACHIO COUSCOUS Combine couscous with the water and butter in large heatproof bowl, cover; stand about 5 minutes or until water is absorbed, fluffing with fork occasionally. Stir in coriander and nuts.

serves 4
per serving 31g total fat (14.7g saturated fat); 3214kJ (769 cal); 76.7g carbohydrate; 45.4g protein; 12.3g fibre

traditional roast dinner

PREPARATION TIME 30 MINUTES **COOKING TIME** 1 HOUR 10 MINUTES

2kg lamb leg

3 sprigs fresh rosemary, chopped coarsely

½ teaspoon sweet paprika

1kg potatoes, chopped coarsely

500g piece pumpkin, chopped coarsely

3 small brown onions (240g), halved

2 tablespoons olive oil

2 tablespoons plain flour

1 cup (250ml) chicken stock

¼ cup (60ml) dry red wine

CAULIFLOWER MORNAY

1 small cauliflower (1kg), cut into florets

50g butter

¼ cup (35g) plain flour

2 cups (500ml) milk

¾ cup (90g) coarsely grated cheddar cheese

1. Preheat oven to moderately hot (200°C/180°C fan-forced).
2. Place lamb in large lightly oiled baking dish; using sharp knife, score skin at 2cm intervals, sprinkle with rosemary and paprika. Roast lamb, uncovered, in moderately hot oven 15 minutes.
3. Reduce heat to moderate (180°C/160°C fan-forced); roast lamb, uncovered, about 45 minutes or until cooked as desired.
4. Meanwhile, place potato, pumpkin and onion, in single layer, in large shallow baking dish; drizzle with oil. Roast, uncovered, in moderate oven for last 45 minutes of lamb cooking time.
5. Make cauliflower mornay.
6. Remove lamb and vegetables from oven; cover to keep warm. Strain pan juices from lamb into medium jug. Return ¼ cup of the pan juices to flameproof dish over medium heat, add flour; cook, stirring, about 5 minutes or until mixture bubbles and browns. Gradually add stock and wine; cook over high heat, stirring, until gravy boils and thickens.
7. Strain gravy; serve with sliced lamb, roasted vegetables and cauliflower mornay.

CAULIFLOWER MORNAY Boil, steam or microwave cauliflower until tender; drain. Melt butter in medium saucepan, add flour; cook, stirring, until mixture bubbles and thickens. Gradually add milk; cook, stirring, until mixture boils and thickens. Stir in half of the cheese. Preheat grill. Place cauliflower in 1.5-litre (6-cup) shallow flameproof dish; pour mornay sauce over cauliflower, sprinkle with remaining cheese. Place under preheated grill about 10 minutes or until browned lightly.

serves 6
per serving 35.6g total fat (17g saturated fat); 3244kJ (776 cal); 40.5g carbohydrate; 71.9g protein; 7g fibre

lamb burgers with beetroot relish and yogurt

PREPARATION TIME 30 MINUTES **COOKING TIME** 45 MINUTES

500g lamb mince

1 small brown onion (80g), chopped finely

2 cloves garlic, crushed

1 teaspoon ground cumin

1 egg, beaten lightly

1 tablespoon olive oil

¾ cup (210g) greek-style yogurt

½ teaspoon ground cumin, extra

1 tablespoon finely chopped fresh mint

1 long loaf pide

50g baby rocket leaves

BEETROOT RELISH

⅓ cup (80ml) water

4 medium beetroots (700g), trimmed, grated coarsely

1 small brown onion (80g), chopped finely

½ cup (110g) white sugar

⅔ cup (160ml) apple cider vinegar

1 Make beetroot relish.

2 Meanwhile, using hand, combine lamb, onion, garlic, cumin and egg in medium bowl; shape mixture into four patties.

3 Heat oil in large frying pan; cook patties, uncovered, until browned both sides and cooked as desired. Cover to keep warm.

4 Combine yogurt, extra cumin and mint in small bowl.

5 Cut pide into quarters; halve quarters horizontally. Toast pide pieces, cut-side up. Sandwich rocket, patties, yogurt mixture and relish between pide pieces.

BEETROOT RELISH Combine the water, beetroot and onion in large non-stick frying pan; cook, covered, about 15 minutes or until beetroot is tender. Stir in sugar and vinegar; cook, covered, stirring occasionally, 20 minutes. Uncover; cook, stirring occasionally, about 10 minutes or until liquid evaporates.

tip Beetroot relish will keep, covered and refrigerated, for up to three days.

serves 4

per serving 22g total fat (7.9g saturated fat); 3173kJ (759 cal); 95.9g carbohydrate; 43.6g protein; 8.6g fibre

lamb shank soup

PREPARATION TIME 40 MINUTES (PLUS STANDING AND REFRIGERATION TIME) **COOKING TIME** 2 HOURS 50 MINUTES

1½ cups (300g) dried chickpeas
1 tablespoon olive oil
1.5kg french-trimmed lamb shanks
1 medium brown onion (150g), chopped finely
2 medium carrots (240g), chopped finely
2 trimmed celery stalks (200g), sliced thinly
2 cloves garlic, crushed
1 teaspoon ground cumin
2 cups (500ml) chicken stock
1 litre (4 cups) water
8 large stalks silverbeet (400g), chopped finely
¼ cup (60ml) lemon juice

1 Place chickpeas in medium bowl, cover with water; stand overnight. Rinse under cold water; drain.
2 Meanwhile, heat oil in large saucepan; cook lamb, in batches, until browned. Cook onion, carrot, celery, garlic and cumin in same pan, stirring, about 5 minutes or until onion softens. Return lamb to pan with stock and the water; bring to a boil. Reduce heat; simmer, covered, 2 hours.
3 Remove soup mixture from heat; when lamb is cool enough to handle, remove meat, chop coarsely. Refrigerate cooled soup mixture and lamb meat, covered separately, overnight.
4 Discard fat from surface of soup mixture. Place soup mixture, meat and chickpeas in large saucepan; bring to a boil. Reduce heat; simmer, covered, 30 minutes. Add silverbeet and lemon; simmer, uncovered, until silverbeet just wilts. Serve soup with a warmed loaf of ciabatta, if desired.

serves 4
per serving 28.2g total fat (9.9g saturated fat); 2654kJ (635 cal); 35.7g carbohydrate; 59.1g protein; 15.6g fibre

Silverbeet is all too often given short shrift over another green leafy vegetable, spinach. Also known as swiss chard or blettes, it's a member of the beet family rather than the spinach family, a fact reflected in the robust texture of its leaves and wide edible stems (which are delicious in their own right). It suits the flavours of the Mediterranean menu – garlic, sultanas, tomato, pine nuts, lemon and olive oil – and it makes a great Turkish soup with lentils, yogurt and lemon juice.

italian cottage pie

PREPARATION TIME 25 MINUTES **COOKING TIME** 1 HOUR

- 1 tablespoon olive oil
- 1 medium brown onion (150g), chopped finely
- 2 cloves garlic, crushed
- 200g mushrooms, sliced thinly
- 1 large carrot (180g), diced into 1cm pieces
- 1 medium eggplant (300g), diced into 1cm pieces
- 750g lamb mince
- 1 tablespoon plain flour
- ½ cup (125ml) dry red wine
- 425g can crushed tomatoes
- 2 tablespoons tomato paste
- 1 tablespoon worcestershire sauce
- 2 tablespoons finely chopped fresh oregano
- 800g potatoes, chopped coarsely
- 20g butter
- ⅓ cup (80ml) milk
- ¼ cup (20g) finely grated parmesan cheese

SOFT POLENTA

- 1¼ cups (310ml) chicken stock
- ¾ cup (180ml) milk
- ½ cup (85g) polenta
- ¼ cup (20g) finely grated parmesan cheese

1 Preheat oven to moderately hot (200°C/180°C fan-forced). Grease deep 2.5-litre (10-cup) casserole dish.

2 Heat oil in large frying pan; cook onion, garlic, mushrooms, carrot and eggplant, stirring, until onion softens. Add lamb; cook, stirring, until browned. Add flour; cook, stirring, 1 minute. Add wine; bring to a boil, stirring. Stir in undrained tomatoes, paste, sauce and oregano. Reduce heat; simmer, uncovered, about 10 minutes or until mixture thickens slightly.

3 Meanwhile, make soft polenta.

4 Boil, steam or microwave potato until tender; drain. Mash potatoes with butter and milk in large bowl until smooth. Using wooden spoon, gently swirl hot polenta mixture into potato mixture.

5 Spoon mince mixture into prepared dish; top with potato polenta mixture, sprinkle with cheese. Cook, uncovered, in moderately hot oven about 25 minutes or until cheese browns lightly.

6 Serve with baby rocket leaves in balsamic vinaigrette, if desired.

SOFT POLENTA Combine stock and milk in large saucepan; bring to a boil. Gradually add polenta to stock mixture, stirring constantly. Reduce heat; cook, stirring, about 10 minutes or until polenta thickens. Stir in cheese.

serves 6

per serving 19.4g total fat (8.8g saturated fat); 2040kJ (488 cal); 37.1g carbohydrate; 37.5g protein; 6.7g fibre

neck chop and lentil stew with kumara and carrot mash

PREPARATION TIME 20 MINUTES **COOKING TIME** 1 HOUR 45 MINUTES

1 cup (200g) brown lentils

1 tablespoon vegetable oil

1.5kg neck chops

2 medium brown onions (300g), chopped coarsely

2 cloves garlic, crushed

4 bacon rashers (280g), rind removed, chopped coarsely

1 teaspoon caraway seeds

2 teaspoons ground cumin

½ cup (125ml) dry red wine

⅓ cup (90g) tomato paste

2 cups (500ml) beef stock

425g can diced tomatoes

½ cup coarsely chopped fresh coriander

KUMARA AND CARROT MASH

2 medium kumara (800g), chopped coarsely

2 medium carrots (240g), chopped coarsely

1 teaspoon ground cumin

⅓ cup (80ml) buttermilk

1. Cook lentils in large saucepan of boiling water, uncovered, about 15 minutes or until tender; drain.
2. Preheat oven to moderate (180°C/160°C fan-forced).
3. Meanwhile, heat oil in large flameproof casserole dish; cook chops, in batches, until browned. Cook onion, garlic and bacon in same heated pan, stirring, until onion is just browned and bacon is crisp. Add spices; cook, stirring, until fragrant. Add wine, paste, stock and undrained tomatoes; bring to a boil.
4. Return chops to dish; stir in lentils, Cook, covered, in moderate oven 1 hour 10 minutes.
5. Meanwhile, make kumara and carrot mash.
6. Stir coriander into stew just before serving with mash.

KUMARA AND CARROT MASH Boil, steam or microwave kumara and carrot, separately, until tender; drain. Dry-fry cumin in small frying pan until fragrant. Mash vegetables in large bowl with cumin and buttermilk until smooth.

serves 4
per serving 47.9g total fat (19.6g saturated fat); 3896kJ (932 cal); 44.2g carbohydrate; 76.1g protein; 9.9g fibre

slow-cooked shank and bean ragout

PREPARATION TIME 30 MINUTES (PLUS STANDING TIME) **COOKING TIME** 2 HOURS 30 MINUTES

Haricot and borlotti beans are just two members of the legume family. From the humble baked bean to the chickpea, legumes contain healthy components linked with protection against diseases such as cancer, diabetes and heart problems. They are high in soluble fibre and low in fat, and best of all, they fill you up without filling you out.

½ cup (100g) dried haricot beans
½ cup (100g) dried borlotti beans
8 french-trimmed lamb shanks (1.6kg)
2 tablespoons plain flour
1 tablespoon olive oil
1 large brown onion (200g), chopped coarsely
1 medium carrot (120g), chopped coarsely
1 trimmed celery stalk (100g), chopped coarsely
1 fresh long red chilli, chopped finely
¼ cup (60ml) balsamic vinegar
425g can crushed tomatoes
8 drained anchovies in oil
½ cup (125ml) dry white wine
1 cup (250ml) water
⅓ cup coarsely chopped fresh flat-leaf parsley

1 Place beans in large bowl, cover with water; stand overnight. Rinse under cold water; drain. Place beans in medium saucepan, cover with boiling water; bring to a boil. Reduce heat; simmer, uncovered, about 15 minutes or until beans are just tender. Drain.
2 Preheat oven to moderate (180°C/160°C fan-forced).
3 Toss lamb in flour; shake away excess. Heat oil in large flameproof casserole dish; cook lamb, in batches, until browned. Cook onion, carrot, celery and chilli in same dish, stirring, about 5 minutes or until onion softens. Return lamb to dish with beans, vinegar, undrained tomatoes, anchovies, wine and the water; bring to a boil. Cook ragout, covered, in moderate oven 1 hour, stirring occasionally. Uncover; cook in moderate oven about 1 hour or until meat is almost falling off the bone. Stir parsley through ragout just before serving.

serves 4
per serving 18.1g total fat (6.5g saturated fat); 2077kJ (497 cal); 24g carbohydrate; 54.9g protein; 5.2g fibre

about lamb

Nutritious, versatile and delicious... no wonder lamb is so universally adored. Here are a few tips and techniques on how to treat this meat to make the most of its qualities.

selecting & storing

Lamb is sold stamped by name on the rind with a red edible dye: this validates its age and place of origin. Any meat sold as lamb not marked in this way could be of dubious quality or from an older animal. Check with your butcher, however, because in some of the newer cuts, it's possible that the brand could have been trimmed away. Look for meat that is a fresh, deep pink colour and has some marbling (veins of fat that keep the meat from drying out during cooking). The fat itself should be firm, dry and an off-white colour. Once home, unwrap the meat and transfer it to a plate or plastic container; cover it loosely so that air can circulate around it then refrigerate it if you intend to consume it within two days. Otherwise, freeze the meat, wrapped tightly to prevent freezer burn and dehydration. Always thaw frozen meat in the refrigerator, not on the kitchen bench.

keep it clean

Keep one plastic cutting board for the exclusive use of raw meat; scrub it well with soap and hot water or run it through your dishwasher after use. You shouldn't use the same knife or board – or your hands – for both raw and cooked meat until they've been washed. All lamb, uncooked and cooked, should be refrigerated until you are ready to start cooking or to sit down to eat. Don't place uncooked lamb above cooked food in your refrigerator in case any juices drip from the raw meat.

the cut's the thing

Eye of loin (backstrap), fillet and trim lamb steaks are tender cuts best cooked rapidly – think barbecuing, char-grilling or pan-frying. Rump or topside mini roasts are also quick-cooking and have little wastage. If you like your meat well done, choose well-marbled lamb to ensure that it remains moist and tender. Forequarter cuts – shanks, chops and shoulder – have the most connective tissue and are best "wet-cooked" – braised, stewed or pot-roasted. As a rule of thumb, dry cooking methods are best for cuts having the least connective tissue.

just like mum's

Making a perfect roast isn't exactly rocket science, but it does take some thought. Be sure your oven is preheated to the desired temperature before the meat goes in. Weigh the roast and estimate its cooking time (see below), then insert a meat thermometer into the thickest part of the meat. Elevate the roast on a metal rack set over a baking dish. Pour a little water into the dish to stop any juices burning, and while the lamb is roasting, baste it occasionally. Add more water to the dish if there's not enough liquid to baste throughout cooking. When the estimated roasting time is reached, check the thermometer to read the internal temperature: the meat will be rare at 60°C; medium at 70°C; and well done at 75°C. Remove the roast from the oven, cover it loosely with foil and let it rest for about 10 or 15 minutes to allow the juices to settle before carving.

cooking times

Lamb rack and **crown roast** require 45 to 55 minutes cooking time at 200°C regardless of weight. Cook **mini roasts** at 220°C for 7 minutes per 100g for rare; 9 minutes per 100g for medium; and 11 minutes per 100g for well done. Cook **neck fillet roast** and **eye of loin** at 220°C for 9 to 10 minutes per 100g for medium and 11 to 12 minutes per 100g for well done. **Leg, shoulder and all other cuts** should be roasted at 180°C for 20 to 25 minutes per 500g for rare; 25 to 30 minutes per 500g for medium; and 30 to 35 minutes per 500g for well done.

glossary

ACIDULATED WATER water to which lemon juice or pulp has been added to prevent the cut surfaces of foods, such as artichokes and apples, from discolouring.

ALLSPICE also known as pimento or jamaican pepper; so-named because it tastes like a combination of nutmeg, cinnamon, cumin and clove – all spices.

ARTICHOKE HEARTS tender centre of the globe artichoke. Purchase fresh, or in brine in glass jars.

BACON RASHERS also known as slices of bacon.

BARLEY a nutritious grain used in soups and stews.

BEANS
black also known as turtle beans. They are not the same as chinese black beans, which are fermented soy beans.
borlotti also known as roman beans.
broad also known as fava, windsor or horse beans. Fresh and frozen are best peeled twice (discard both the outer long green pod and the beige-green tough inner shell).
cannelloni, haricot, navy, great northern all small, white, dried beans. Soak first in water before use.

BEAN SPROUTS also known as bean shoots.

BOK CHOY also called pak choi or chinese white cabbage; has a fresh, mild mustard taste. *Baby bok choy* is slightly more tender than bok choy.

BREADCRUMBS
packaged fine-textured, crunchy, purchased white breadcrumbs.
stale one- or two-day-old bread made into crumbs by blending or processing.

BUTTER use salted or unsalted ("sweet") butter; 125g is equal to one stick of butter.

BUTTERMILK originally the liquid left after cream was separated from milk, today it is commercially made similarly to yogurt. Sold in the refrigerated section in supermarkets.

BUTTERNUT PUMPKIN pear-shaped with golden skin and orange flesh.

CAPERS the grey-green buds of a warm climate (usually Mediterranean) shrub, sold either dried and salted or pickled in a vinegar brine. *Baby capers* are smaller and more flavoursome – and more expensive – than the full-sized ones. Rinse well before using.

CAPSICUM also known as bell pepper or, simply, pepper. Discard seeds and membranes before use.

CHEESE
bocconcini walnut-sized baby mozzarella made from buffalo milk. Spoils rapidly so must be kept under refrigeration, in brine, for 1 or 2 days.
fetta a crumbly goat- or sheep-milk cheese with a sharp salty taste.
haloumi a firm, cream-coloured sheep-milk cheese matured in brine; somewhat like a minty, salty fetta in flavour.
pizza a commercial blend of processed grated mozzarella, cheddar and parmesan.

CHAR SUI SAUCE also called chinese barbecue sauce; has a sweet, spicy flavour. Made with honey, fermented soy beans and various spices.

CHILLIES use rubber gloves when seeding and chopping fresh chillies to prevent burning your skin.
flakes dried, deep-red, dehydrated chilli slices and whole seeds.
thai red small, bright red and very hot; substitute with fresh serrano or habanero chillies.

CHINESE RICE WINE a clear distillation of fermented rice, water and salt, about 29.5% alcohol by volume; used for marinades and sauces.

CHOY SUM also known as pakaukeo or flowering cabbage, a member of the bok choy family; easy to identify with its long stems, light green leaves and yellow flowers. Is eaten, stems and all, steamed or stir-fried.

COS LETTUCE also known as romaine lettuce.

CHICKPEAS a sandy-coloured legume also known as garbanzos, channa or hummus.

CORIANDER also known as cilantro or chinese parsley; bright-green leafy herb with pungent flavour. Also sold as seeds, whole or ground.

CORNFLOUR also known as cornstarch; used as a thickening agent in all types of cooking.

EGG some recipes call for raw or barely cooked eggs; exercise caution if there's a salmonella problem in your area.

EGGPLANT also known as aubergine.

EYE OF LOIN also sold as lamb backstrap.

FISH SAUCE also called nam pla or nuoc nam; made from pulverised, salted, fermented fish, most often anchovies.

FIVE-SPICE POWDER fragrant ground mixture of cinnamon, clove, star anise, sichuan pepper and fennel seeds.

FLAT-LEAF PARSLEY also known as continental or italian parsley.

FLOUR, PLAIN all-purpose flour, made from wheat.

GAI LARN also known as gai lum, chinese broccoli or chinese kale. Stems are more edible than leaves.

GARAM MASALA a spice blend of cardamom, cinnamon, cloves, cumin, coriander and fennel.

GINGER also known as green or root ginger; cannot be substituted with powered ginger.

HARISSA a North African paste made from dried red chillies, garlic, olive oil and caraway seeds.

HOISIN SAUCE a thick, sweet and spicy Chinese paste made from salted fermented soy beans, onions and garlic.

KALAMATA OLIVES small, sharp-tasting, red-wine-brine-cured black olives.

KECAP MANIS also known as ketjap manis; a thick soy sauce with added sugar and spices.

KUMARA Polynesian name of orange-fleshed sweet potato, often confused with yam.

LEBANESE CUCUMBER short, thin-skinned and slender; also known as the european or burpless cucumber.

MINCE also known as ground meat; we used lamb mince unless stated otherwise.

MIRIN SWEET RICE WINE used in Japanese cooking; not to be confused with sake, the Japanese rice wine made for drinking.

MIZUNA a wispy, green salad leaf that originated in Japan.

MUSHROOMS
button small, cultivated white mushrooms with a mild flavour.
shiitake when fresh are also known as chinese black, forest or golden oak mushrooms. Are large and meaty; often used as a substitute for meat in some Asian vegetarian dishes. When dried, they are known as donko or dried chinese mushrooms; rehydrate before use.

swiss brown light to dark brown mushrooms also known as roman or cremini. Can be substituted with button or cap mushrooms.

MUSTARD, DIJON a pale brown, distinctively flavoured, fairly mild french mustard.

NAAN round, leavened bread associated with the tandoori dishes of northern India; traditionally baked pressed against the inside wall of a heated tandoor or clay oven.

NOODLES
hokkien also known as stir-fry noodles; fresh wheat noodles resembling thick, yellow-brown spaghetti, no precooking needed before use.
rice soft white noodles made from rice flour and vegetable oil; available in varying thicknesses. Rinse under hot water before using.

PALM SUGAR also known as nam tan pip, jaggery, jawa or gula melaka; made from the sap of sugar cane and palm trees. Light brown to black in colour; usually sold in rock-hard cakes; substitute with brown sugar, if unavailable.

PAPRIKA ground dried red capsicum; available sweet or hot.

PIDE also known as turkish bread. Comes in long (about 45cm) flat loaves as well as individual rounds; made from wheat flour and sprinkled with sesame or black onion seeds.

PINE NUTS also known as pignoli.

PITTA also known as lebanese bread; is sold in large, flat pieces that separate into two thin rounds. Also available in small thick pieces called pocket pitta.

POLENTA also known as cornmeal; a flour-like cereal made of dried corn (maize). Sold ground in different textures; also the name of the dish made from it.

PRESERVED LEMON a North African specialty, the citrus is preserved, usually whole, in a mixture of salt and lemon juice. Can be rinsed and eaten as is, or added to casseroles and tagines to impart a rich salty-sour acidic flavour.

PROSCIUTTO cured, air-dried, pressed ham; usually sold thinly sliced.

QUINCE yellow-skinned fruit with hard texture and astringent, tart taste; eaten cooked or as a preserve.

RICE
arborio small, round-grain rice well suited to absorb a large amount of liquid.
basmati white, fragrant long-grain rice usually associated with the food of India.

ROCKET also known as arugula, rugula or rucola; a peppery-tasting green leaf that can be used similarly to baby spinach leaves, eaten raw in salads or used in cooking. *Baby rocket leaves* are both smaller and less peppery.

SAFFRON stigma of a member of the crocus family; imparts a yellow-orange colour to food once infused. Available in strands or ground form; should be stored in the freezer.

SALSA the Spanish word for sauce. A typical Mexican raw sauce is called salsa cruda; one made with green tomatoes or any combination of all-green herbs or vegetables is called salsa verde.

SAKE rice wine used in cooking, marinating, as part of dipping sauces and as a drink. Substitute dry sherry or brandy.

SAMBAL OELEK also ulek or olek. Indonesian in origin; a salty paste made from ground chillies.

SHALLOTS also called french shallots, golden shallots or eschalots; small, brown-skinned members of the onion family. Grows in tight clusters similarly to garlic.

SILVERBEET also known as swiss chard or chard; a leafy, dark green vegetable, related to the beet, with thick, crisp white or red stems and ribs. The leaves, often trimmed from the stems and ribs, are used raw or cooked.

SNOW PEAS also called mange tout ("eat all"). Snow pea tendrils, the growing shoots of the plant, are sold by greengrocers.

SPRING ONION immature onion with a small, white, walnut-sized bulb and long green leaves; larger version of green onion.

SUGAR SNAP PEAS also known as honey snap peas; fresh small peas that can be eaten whole, pod and all, similarly to snow peas.

STAR ANISE a dried, star-shaped fruit of a tree native to China. The pod, which has an astringent aniseed taste, is used to flavour stocks and marinades.

SUMAC a purple-red, astringent spice with a tart, lemony flavour; found in Middle-Eastern food stores. *Substitute:* ½ teaspoon lemon pepper *plus* ⅛ teaspoon five-spice *plus* ⅛ teaspoon allspice *equals* ¾ teaspoon sumac.

TAMARI a thick, dark soy sauce made mainly from soy beans without the wheat used in standard soy sauce.

TAMARIND CONCENTRATE (or paste) commercial distillation of tamarind pulp into a condensed paste. No soaking or straining required, but can be diluted with water according to taste.

TAPENADE a thick, black paste containing black olives, olive oil, capers, anchovies as well as Mediterranean herbs. Used as an ingredient in dressings and sauces, or eaten on its own as a spread or dip.

TAT SOI a variety of bok choy also known as tai gu choy, rosette pak choy or chinese flat cabbage. Its dark green leaves are cut into sections, rather than separated, and used in soups and stir-fries.

THAI BASIL has smallish leaves and a sweet licorice/aniseed taste; it is one of the basic flavours that typify Thai cuisine. Available in Asian supermarkets and greengrocers.

TOMATO PASTA SAUCE, BOTTLED a prepared sauce made from a blend of tomatoes, herbs and spices.

TORTILLA thin, round, unleavened bread originating in Mexico. Two kinds are available, one made from wheat flour and the other from corn.

VIETNAMESE MINT also known as cambodian mint or laksa leaf; a narrow-leafed, pungent herb.

ZA'ATAR a dry blend of roasted sesame seeds, wild marjoram, thyme and sumac; available from Middle-Eastern specialty food shops.

conversion chart

measures

One Australian metric measuring cup holds approximately 250ml, one Australian metric tablespoon holds 20ml, one Australian metric teaspoon holds 5ml.

The difference between one country's measuring cups and another's is within a two- or three-teaspoon variance, and will not affect your cooking results. North America, New Zealand and the United Kingdom use a 15ml tablespoon.

All cup and spoon measurements are level. The most accurate way of measuring dry ingredients is to weigh them. When measuring liquids, use a clear glass or plastic jug with the metric markings.

We use large eggs with an average weight of 60g.

dry measures

METRIC	IMPERIAL
15g	½oz
30g	1oz
60g	2oz
90g	3oz
125g	4oz (¼lb)
155g	5oz
185g	6oz
220g	7oz
250g	8oz (½lb)
280g	9oz
315g	10oz
345g	11oz
375g	12oz (¾lb)
410g	13oz
440g	14oz
470g	15oz
500g	16oz (1lb)
750g	24oz (1½lb)
1kg	32oz (2lb)

liquid measures

METRIC	IMPERIAL
30ml	1 fluid oz
60ml	2 fluid oz
100ml	3 fluid oz
125ml	4 fluid oz
150ml	5 fluid oz (¼ pint/1 gill)
190ml	6 fluid oz
250ml	8 fluid oz
300ml	10 fluid oz (½ pint)
500ml	16 fluid oz
600ml	20 fluid oz (1 pint)
1000ml (1 litre)	1¾ pints

length measures

METRIC	IMPERIAL
3mm	⅛in
6mm	¼in
1cm	½in
2cm	¾in
2.5cm	1in
5cm	2in
6cm	2½in
8cm	3in
10cm	4in
13cm	5in
15cm	6in
18cm	7in
20cm	8in
23cm	9in
25cm	10in
28cm	11in
30cm	12in (1ft)

oven temperatures

These oven temperatures are only a guide for conventional ovens. For fan-forced ovens, check the manufacturer's manual.

	°C (CELSIUS)	°F (FAHRENHEIT)	GAS MARK
Very slow	120	250	½
Slow	150	275-300	1-2
Moderately slow	160	325	3
Moderate	180	350-375	4-5
Moderately hot	200	400	6
Hot	220	425-450	7-8
Very hot	240	475	9

index

ARE YOU MISSING SOME OF THE WORLD'S FAVOURITE COOKBOOKS?

The Australian Women's Weekly Cookbooks are available from bookshops, cookshops, supermarkets and other stores all over the world. You can also buy direct from the publisher, using the order form below.

TITLE	RRP	QTY	TITLE	RRP	QTY
Asian, Meals in Minutes	£6.99		Indian Cooking Class	£6.99	
Babies & Toddlers Good Food	£6.99		Japanese Cooking Class	£6.99	
Barbecue Meals In Minutes	£6.99		Just For One (Feb 07)	£6.99	
Beginners Cooking Class	£6.99		Kids' Birthday Cakes	£6.99	
Beginners Simple Meals	£6.99		Kids Cooking	£6.99	
Beginners Thai	£6.99		Kids' Cooking Step-by-Step	£6.99	
Best Food	£6.99		Lean Food	£6.99	
Best Food Desserts	£6.99		Low-carb, Low-fat	£6.99	
Best Food Fast	£6.99		Low-fat Feasts	£6.99	
Best Food Mains	£6.99		Low-fat Food For Life	£6.99	
Cafe Classics	£6.99		Low-fat Meals in Minutes	£6.99	
Cakes Biscuits & Slices	£6.99		Main Course Salads	£6.99	
Cakes Cooking Class	£6.99		Mexican	£6.99	
Caribbean Cooking	£6.99		Middle Eastern Cooking Class	£6.99	
Casseroles	£6.99		Midweek Meals in Minutes	£6.99	
Casseroles & Slow-Cooked Classics	£6.99		Moroccan & the Foods of North Africa	£6.99	
Cheap Eats (Feb 07)	£6.99		Muffins, Scones & Breads	£6.99	
Cheesecakes: baked and chilled	£6.99		New Casseroles	£6.99	
Chicken	£6.99		New Classics	£6.99	
Chicken Meals in Minutes	£6.99		New Curries	£6.99	
Chinese Cooking Class	£6.99		New Finger Food	£6.99	
Christmas Cooking	£6.99		New Salads	£6.99	
Chocolate	£6.99		Party Food and Drink	£6.99	
Cocktails	£6.99		Pasta Meals in Minutes	£6.99	
Cooking for Friends	£6.99		Potatoes	£6.99	
Cupcakes & Fairycakes	£6.99		Salads: Simple, Fast & Fresh	£6.99	
Detox	£6.99		Saucery	£6.99	
Dinner Beef	£6.99		Sauces Salsas & Dressings	£6.99	
Dinner Lamb	£6.99		Sensational Stir-Fries	£6.99	
Dinner Seafood	£6.99		Slim	£6.99	
Easy Curry	£6.99		Stir-fry	£6.99	
Easy Spanish-Style	£6.99		Superfoods for Exam Success	£6.99	
Essential Soup	£6.99		Sweet Old Fashioned Favourites	£6.99	
Foods That Fight Back	£6.99		Tapas Mezze Antipasto & other bites	£6.99	
French Food, New	£6.99		Thai Cooking Class	£6.99	
Fresh Food Fast	£6.99		Traditional Italian	£6.99	
Fresh Food for Babies & Toddlers	£6.99		Vegetarian Meals in Minutes	£6.99	
Good Food Fast	£6.99		Vegie Food	£6.99	
Great Lamb Cookbook	£6.99		Wicked Sweet Indulgences	£6.99	
Greek Cooking Class	£6.99		Wok, Meals in Minutes	£6.99	
Grills	£6.99				
Healthy Heart Cookbook	£6.99		TOTAL COST:	£	

ACP Magazines Ltd
Privacy Notice
This book may contain offers, competitions or surveys that require you to provide information about yourself if you choose to enter or take part in any such Reader Offer. If you provide information about yourself to ACP Magazines Ltd, the company will use this information to provide you with the products or services you have requested, and may supply your information to contractors that help ACP to do this. ACP will also use your information to inform you of other ACP publications, products, services and events. ACP will also give your information to organisations that are providing special prizes or offers, and that are clearly associated with the Reader Offer. Unless you tell us not to, we may give your information to other organisations that use it to inform you about other products, services and events or who may give it to other organisations that may use it for this purpose. If you would like to gain access to the information ACP holds about you, please contact ACP's Privacy Officer at ACP Magazines Ltd, 54-58 Park Street, Sydney, NSW 2000, Australia.

☐ **Privacy Notice**
Please do not provide information about me to any organisation not associated with this offer.

Mr/Mrs/Ms ______________________________

Address ______________________________

______________________ Postcode ____________

Day time phone ____________ Email* (optional) ____________

I enclose my cheque/money order for £ ______________

or please charge £ ______________

to my: ☐ Access ☐ Mastercard ☐ Visa ☐ Diners Club

PLEASE NOTE: WE DO NOT ACCEPT SWITCH OR ELECTRON CARDS

Card number | | | | | | | | | | | | | | | | |

Expiry date ________ 3 digit security code *(found on reverse of card)* ______

Cardholder's name ______________ Signature ______________

* By including your email address, you consent to receipt of any email regarding this magazine, and other emails which inform you of ACP's other publications, products, services and events, and to promote third party goods and services you may be interested in.

To order: Mail or fax – photocopy or complete the order form above, and send your credit card details or cheque payable to: Australian Consolidated Press (UK), Moulton Park Business Centre, Red House Road, Moulton Park, Northampton NN3 6AQ, phone (+44) (0) 1604 497531 fax (+44) (0) 1604 497533, e-mail books@acpuk.com or order online at www.acpuk.com

Non-UK residents: We accept the credit cards listed on the coupon, or cheques, drafts or International Money Orders payable in sterling and drawn on a UK bank. Credit card charges are at the exchange rate current at the time of payment.

Postage and packing UK: Add £1.00 per order plus 50p per book.

Postage and packing overseas: Add £2.00 per order plus £1.00 per book.

All pricing current at time of going to press and subject to change/availability.

Offer ends 31.12.2007